PLAY BALL!

Over 1011 baseball fun facts and trivia questions for baseball fans of all ages!

Walter Beede

Contents

Introduction

I would like to welcome you to the thrilling world of baseball, where each game is a new opportunity to see the remarkable and the unexpected. There is nothing quite like the experience of going to a live baseball game. From the sight of the green grass, the sound of the crack of the bat to the roar of the crowd, there is nothing quite like it. Yet even if you aren't a die-hard fan, there are still many things about this time-honored American activity that you may appreciate.

You probably weren't aware of this, but in the early days of baseball, the pitcher had to throw the ball underhanded. Amos Rusie, a pitcher, changed all of that in the late 1800s when he devised an overhand pitching style that completely transformed the game. Rusie was renowned for his amazing speed, and he held the record for the fastest pitch ever thrown, clocking in at almost 100 miles per hour! This record remained for more than a century.

The New York Yankees are widely regarded as one of the most legendary teams in the history of baseball. The Yankees have been responsible for producing some of the game's most renowned players, including Babe Ruth and Derek Jeter. But were you aware that there was a real possibility that the squad might never be formed? In 1901, a group of businessmen purchased the Baltimore Orioles, relocated the club to New York, and renamed it the New York Highlanders. The team played under this name until 1913. The Yankees quickly became one of the most storied professional teams of all time! The franchise eventually rose to become one of the most successful in the history of baseball.

Baseball is also well-known for the peculiar customs and superstitions that are associated with the sport. Take, for example, the career of Wade Boggs, who formerly played third base for the Boston Red Sox. Boggs was well-known for his peculiar pre-game ritual, which consisted of always eating chicken before each game. Before each at-bat, he would write the word "Chick" in the dirt. This was his trademark strategy. Boggs had a spectacular career, garnering 12 All-Star selections and a spot in the Baseball Hall of Fame. Whether it was the chicken or just his innate skill, this led to Boggs' incredible accomplishments.

The intriguing world of baseball is the subject of this book, and our mission is to both entertain and inform readers about it. We hope that regardless matter whether you are interested in history, sports, or are just seeking a fun and interesting read, you will find it enjoyable to learn about the many different aspects of this well-loved sport. Thus, grab a hot dog and a cool drink, and get comfortable because you are about to go on an entertaining and educational adventure through the world of baseball stories and amusing facts!

CHAPTER ONE

Baseball Teams

Baseball is famous for its historic clubs, each of which has its own rich past, long-standing customs, and devoted fan base. In this section, we'll take a deeper look at each of the thirty clubs that make up Major League Baseball.

Division of the American League

The Baltimore Orioles are a Major League Baseball team that was established in 1901. Throughout the years, the Orioles have gone on to win three World Series titles and have been home to many notable players, including Cal Ripken Jr. and Brooks Robinson.

The Boston Red Sox are renowned for their ardent and devoted fan following and were founded in 1901. They have won nine championships in the World Series throughout the course of their history.

The New York Yankees are one of the most famous teams in the history of baseball. The Yankees have won 27 World Series victories and have had notable players such as Babe Ruth, Lou Gehrig, and Derek Jeter on their roster. The team was established in 1901.

The Tampa Bay Rays are a Major League Baseball team that was established in 1998 and have competed in one World Series. The Rays are well-known for their creative and analytics-driven approach to the game of baseball.

The Toronto Blue Jays are the only professional baseball club to be founded in Canada. The franchise was established in 1977 and has since gone on to win two World Series titles.

Central Division of the American League

Chicago White Sox: The White Sox franchise was established in 1901, and the team is famed for its colorful history, which includes the infamous Black Sox incident that occurred in 1919. The White Sox have won three World Series victories.

The Cleveland Indians were established in 1901, and they have since gone on to become famous both for the fervent support of their fans and for the historic status of their ballpark, Progressive Field. The Indians have won two World Series titles.

The Detroit Tigers were established in 1894 and have gone on to become one of the most successful baseball teams in history, having won four World Series titles and being famous for having produced such legendary players as Ty Cobb and Al Kaline.

The Kansas City Royals have a reputation for being gritty and taking an underdog attitude to the game. The franchise was established in 1969, and the Royals have since won two World Series victories.

The Minnesota Twins are a major league baseball team that was established in 1901. They have three World Series titles to their name and are famous for having produced such legendary players as Harmon Killebrew and Kirby Puckett.

West of the American League

Houston Astros: The Astros have been to the World Series three times since the franchise's founding in 1962. The Astros are noted for their high-powered offense and powerful pitching staff.

The Los Angeles Angels are a Major League Baseball team that was established in 1961. The Angels have competed in the World Series once, and their most famous player, Mike Trout, is often regarded as the finest player in all of baseball.

The Oakland Athletics are noted for their creative approach to the game, especially their use of sophisticated analytics. The Athletics were founded in 1901 and have gone on to win nine World Series titles.

The Seattle Mariners have never been champions of the World Series, but the franchise is famous for its devoted fan base and legendary players like Ken Griffey Jr. and Ichiro Suzuki. The Mariners were established in 1977.

The Texas Rangers are a professional baseball team that was established in 1961 and have competed in two World Series. The Rangers are well-known for their powerful offense and strong bullpen.

League East of the National

The Atlanta Braves were established in 1871, and they have won three World Series victories since that time. The Braves are famous for having produced such legendary players as Hank Aaron and Chipper Jones.

The Miami Marlins are a baseball team that was established in 1993 and have since gone on to win two World Series titles. The Marlins are famous for their gritty, underdog style of play.

The New York Mets are a major league baseball team that was established in 1962. They have two World Series titles to their name and are famous for their fervent fan base and legendary players, such as Tom Seaver and Michael Piazza.

The Philadelphia Phillies is a major league baseball team that was established in 1883. They have two World Series titles to their name and are famous for their ardent fan base and legendary players, such as Mike Schmidt and Steve Carlton.

The Montreal Expos became the Washington Nationals in 1969 when the franchise was first established.

The Nationals relocated to Washington, District of Columbia. 2005, and they have recently taken home their first World Series title in 2019. The pitching staff of this club is well-known for their dominance, and it features notable players like Max Scherzer and Juan Soto.

Central Division of the National League

The Chicago Cubs are one of the oldest and most renowned baseball clubs, having been founded in 1876. They have won three World Series victories, including a historic triumph in 2016 that broke a 108-year championship drought.

The Cincinnati Reds are an American professional baseball team that was established in 1882. The Reds have won five World Series titles and are famous for producing classic players such as Johnny Bench and Pete Rose.

Milwaukee Brewers: The Brewers have never been champions of the World Series, but the franchise is famous for its ardent fan base and legendary players like Robin Yount and Ryan Braun. The Brewers were established in 1969.

The Pittsburgh Pirates are a professional baseball team that was established in 1881. They have five World Series titles to their name and are famous for having produced such legendary players as Honus Wagner and Roberto Clemente.

The St. Louis Cardinals are one of the most successful teams in the history of baseball. The Cardinals have won 11 World Series victories and have been home to legendary players such as Stan Musial and Albert Pujols. The franchise was established in 1882.

We're in the National League West.

The Arizona Diamondbacks are a professional baseball team that was established in 1998. Since then, they have competed in and won one World Series championship. The Diamondbacks are famous for having a formidable pitching staff that includes Randy Johnson and Curt Schilling.

The Colorado Rockies have never been champions of the World Series, but they are well-known for their high-powered offense as well as their one-of-a-kind home, Coors Field. The Rockies franchise was established in 1993.

The Los Angeles Dodgers are one of the most famous teams in baseball history. The team was established in 1883 and has won six World Series victories in the city of Los Angeles alone. Some of the franchise's most famous players include Jackie Robinson and Sandy Koufax.

San Diego Padres: The Padres have never been champions of the World Series, but the franchise is famous for its ardent fan base and legendary players like Tony Gwynn and Trevor Hoffman. The Padres were established in 1969.

San Francisco Giants: The Giants were founded in 1883 as the New York Gotham's. They have won eight World Series championships, including three in the last decade, and are known for their incredible pitching staff, which includes Christy Mathewson and Madison Bumgarner. In addition, the Giants have won three World Series championships in the last decade.

In conclusion, baseball clubs have been an important part in the development of the game throughout its history, with each team leaving behind its own distinct heritage and customs. There is nothing quite like the feeling you get when you cheer on your favorite team, regardless of whether you are a die-hard fan or a casual watcher of the game. In the next section, we'll take a more in-depth look at some of the most renowned players in the game's history.

Chapter Two

The development of baseball

Baseball is a sport that has a long and illustrious history, one that spans more than one hundred years. Throughout that span of time, both the game and its associated gear have been subjected to major revisions. In this chapter, we will discuss the development of baseball equipment, the first official game of baseball, and the influence that World War II had on the sport.

The Development of Baseball Gear Over the Years

From its conception, baseball has seen a substantial amount of equipment evolution throughout its history. In its earlier forms, the sport was played with a ball made of a pliable substance such as rubber, and the participants did not wear gloves. Together with the development of the game itself came advancements in the associated gaming gear.

Since the beginning of the game, baseball bats have gone through a number of different versions. At the middle of the 19th century, baseballs had a leather cover and a firm cork center when they were originally manufactured. The size of the ball, as well as its weight, grew and shrunk throughout time. The baseball was made smaller towards the beginning of the 1900s in an effort to boost the amount of home runs. In the 1920s, in an effort to boost scoring, the ball was given more bounce.

The core of a modern baseball is constructed of cork and rubber, and it is then wrapped in yarn before being coated in leather.

Even gloves have been subjected to a substantial amount of evolution. During the game's formative years, participants protected their hands with basic leather gloves that offered just a semblance of safety. In the 1870s, the first catcher's mitts were created, and by the early 1900s, gloves had established themselves as an indispensable piece of equipment for every player. During the 1940s and 1950s, baseball gloves expanded in size and gained padding, making them better at protecting players while they were out on the field. Modern gloves are constructed using cutting-edge technology and materials, which allow for more dexterity and dexterity while maintaining optimal protection.

The evolution of bats has also taken place. The first baseball bats were made of wood and were rather thick and hefty. The bats underwent a number of changes as the game progressed. In the 1920s, the diameter of the bat was made smaller, and a spherical shape was mandated for it. The first aluminum bats appeared in the 1970s, and by the 1990s, composite bats had established themselves as the industry standard. These newly developed varieties of bats are lighter and more aerodynamic than their predecessors, which enables players to swing more quickly and drive the ball further.

The very first game of baseball ever played.

In the first ever official game of baseball, which took place on June 19, 1846, the New York Nine faced off against the Knickerbocker Base Ball Club. There were a few hundred people in attendance at the game, which took place in Hoboken, in the state of New Jersey. The game's regulations were quite similar to those of current baseball, although there were a few significant variances. For instance, the pitcher was compelled to throw the ball underhand, and there was no such thing as a strike or ball call during the game. The result of the game was 23-1 in favor of the New York Nine.

The War's Effects on Baseball During World War Two

Baseball was significantly altered because of World War II. A significant number of players were forced into military service, and a few of them even perished while serving their country. Women were recruited to play professional baseball in a league named the All-American Ladies Professional Baseball League to preserve the sport and ensure its continued existence. At a trying period in the history of the United States, the league was in operation from 1943 through 1954, and it was instrumental in preserving the game.

The baseball equipment that was utilized during games was also affected by the conflict. Because there was a lack of metal, there was also a shortage of wood, which led to a reduction in the overall quality of bats. As a direct consequence of this, players were compelled to utilize bats constructed from softer woods, which were inherently weaker and less durable.

Conclusion

In conclusion, both the game of baseball and its equipment have been subjected to a great deal of change over the course of its history. The game has developed into what it is today from its beginnings as a game played with rubber balls and without gloves to its current state, which has composite bats and more sophisticated gloves. The first formal game of baseball was played in 1846, which set the groundwork for the game's future. World War II had a huge influence on the game, which led to the establishment of the All-American Girls Professional Baseball League as well as improvements in the equipment that is used in the game. The game of baseball is always developing and adapting, and it will be fascinating to observe how the sport and its apparatus continue to advance in the years to come. In the following chapter, we'll have a more in-depth discussion of some of the most renowned players in the annals of baseball history.

CHAPTER THREE

Baseball Players

Players have always played a significant role in the development of baseball, and many of them have gone on to achieve legendary status in their own right. In this chapter, we will take a more in-depth look at some of the most legendary players in the history of baseball. These players include Babe Ruth, Jackie Robinson, Willie Mays, and Derek Jeter, among others.

The Great Babe Ruth: A Legend in His Own Time

There is a consensus among baseball fans that Babe Ruth was one of the best players the game has ever seen. Ruth was born in Baltimore in 1895, and he made his debut in the major leagues with the Boston Red Sox in 1914, pitching for the team. After being moved to the New York Yankees in 1919, he quickly rose to prominence as a batter for the club, helping them win seven American League pennants and four World Series titles.

The influence that Ruth had on the game was immense. He was the first player in baseball history to hit more than 30 home runs in a single season and the first player to smash more than 60 home runs in a season. Throughout the course of his career, he established a number of records, one of which was the career home run mark of 714, which was unsurpassed for more than half a century.

Yet, Ruth was much more than just a talented athlete. His demeanor was bigger than life, and he was well-known for his efforts in the charitable sector. Throughout his career, he was instrumental in raising funds for a variety of organizations and charities, and up to the year 1948, when he passed away, he was a well-liked figure in the baseball world.

The "Called Shot" that Babe Ruth took during the 1932 World Series is one of the most well-known legends about the baseball legend. The story goes that Babe Ruth would point to center field before he would hit a home run in that same location. Even though the narrative's veracity has been called into question over the course of its existence, this particular moment in baseball's past is still widely celebrated.

Jackie Robinson, who broke down barriers based on race

Jackie Robinson is yet another significant character in the history of baseball. Robinson, who was born in Georgia in 1919, became the first player of any race to play in Major League Baseball after signing with the Brooklyn Dodgers in 1947. Throughout his career, he was subjected to a great amount of racial prejudice, yet he continued to be a pioneer for civil rights and the integration of sports.

The influence that Robinson had on baseball extended well beyond his achievements on the field. He made advantage of his position to campaign for racial equality and social justice, and his influence as a pioneer in the movement for civil rights is still felt to this day. Robinson was honored with induction into the Baseball Hall of Fame in 1962 and continues to serve as a source of motivation for athletes as well as campaigners.

In 1947, Robinson was subjected to racist comments and abuse by the Philadelphia Phillies manager, Ben Chapman. This incident is one of the most iconic incidents in Robinson's career. Robinson's response was to have one of the finest games of his career, during which he contributed to the Dodgers' victory by hitting four hits in four at-bats.

Willie Mays "THE SAY HEY KID"

Willie Mays is largely considered to be one of the best players in the history of baseball, regardless of position. Mays was born in Alabama in 1931, and he started his professional career with the New York Giants in 1951. He rose to prominence as a player very rapidly, becoming famous for his extraordinary defensive skills, lightning-fast speed, and powerful striking.

The contributions that Mays made to the game were considerable. He was awarded the Most Valuable Player of the National League twice, as well as 12 Gold Gloves, and he was selected for 24 All-Star teams. It was during the 1954 World Series that he made the grab that made him famous. He ran full speed and made an over-the-shoulder catch to prevent Cleveland's Vic Wertz from gaining extra bases. The catch is widely regarded as one of the most iconic and memorable events in the history of baseball.

Mays was well recognized for his likable nature and the passion he had for baseball when he was not on the field. The baseball community continues to hold him in high regard, and his accomplishments continue to serve as a source of motivation for up-and-coming players.

Derek Jeter is now serving as the Yankees' captain.

Derek Jeter is widely regarded as one of the most popular players in the history of the New York Yankees. Jeter was born in New Jersey in 1974, and he started his professional baseball career with the Yankees in 1995. He rapidly established himself as a fan favorite, being famous for his clutch hitting and his ability to lead.

The influence that Jeter had on the game was substantial. He was selected to play for the All-Star squad 14 times and was a part of the Yankees club that won the World Series five times. In addition to that, he was awarded five Gold Gloves and five Silver Sluggers. It is generally agreed that Jeter is one of the best shortstops in the annals of baseball's long history.

Jeter was well respected off the field for the professionalism he displayed and the dedication he showed to the sport. Both his colleagues and his opponents respected him tremendously during his time as captain of the Yankees, a position he held for a total of 12 years. In Game 4 of the 2001 World Series, Derek Jeter blasted a game-winning home run, giving him the moniker "Mr. November" in the process. This performance helped Jeter solidify his image as a player who excels under pressure.

In 2014, when Derek Jeter played his farewell game at Yankee Stadium, it was an emotional event for both the spectators and the players. At a pregame ceremony, both Jeter's old teammates and opponents paid tribute to him in front of the crowd by getting up to give him a standing ovation. He went out as one of baseball's most beloved and respected players, and he retired with that reputation.

Conclusion

Each of the baseball players described in this chapter had a significant and long-lasting influence on the sport they played, and the history of baseball would not be the same without their contributions. These players have earned their place in baseball lore for a variety of reasons, including Babe Ruth's larger-than-life personality, Jackie Robinson's pioneering efforts in breaking the color barrier, Willie Mays' amazing defensive talents, and Derek Jeter's clutch performances and leadership. Their influence on the sport will be felt by subsequent generations for a very long time to come.

CHAPTER FOUR

The Collegiate and Major League Baseball Records

Baseball is a game that relies heavily on statistics, and collegiate and Major League Baseball players and coaches have established some of the most spectacular records in the sport. In this chapter, we'll take a closer look at some of the most impressive records in the history of baseball. Some of these records include the most home runs in a single season, the pitcher with the most strikeouts in a game, the longest hitting streak in Major League Baseball history, and the most stolen bases in a single season, as well as other notable records.

The Single-Season Record for the Most Home Runs Hit

Pete Incaviglia, who played for Oklahoma State University in 1985 and hit 48 home runs during that season, now holds the record for the most home runs in a single season in college baseball. He set the record in 1985. Barry Bonds, who was playing for the San Francisco Giants in 2001 when he hit 73 home runs, is the current holder of the record in Major League Baseball. Bonds' record has been the subject of debate because of allegations that he used performance-enhancing drugs, but it is undeniable that he accomplished an extraordinary achievement.

Babe Ruth's career home run record stands at 714, while Hank Aaron's career home run record stands at 755 and Barry Bonds' career home run record is at 762. Other important home run records in baseball history include these three.

The Pitcher with the Most Strikeouts in a nine-inning game.

Kerry Wood now holds the record for the most strikeouts in a single game in college baseball. In 1998, while playing for the University of Texas, Wood struck out 20 hitters in a single game, setting the record. Both Roger Clemens and Kerry Wood hold the record for the most hitters struck out in a single game in the history of Major League Baseball (MLB). Clemens was able to accomplish this accomplishment not once, but twice: the first time, in 1986, he did it while pitching against the Seattle Mariners, and the second time, in 1996, he did it while pitching against the Detroit Tigers.

Nolan Ryan's career record of 5,714 strikeouts, Cy Young's career record of 511 wins, and Mariano Rivera's career record of 652 saves are three more important pitching marks in the annals of baseball history.

The Major League Baseball record for the Longest Hitting Streak

Joe DiMaggio now holds the record for the longest hitting skid in the history of Major League Baseball (MLB). In 1941, while playing for the New York Yankees, DiMaggio went hitless in 56 straight games. This record has been in place for over eighty years and is usually considered to be among the most remarkable records in the history of all sports. During the record-setting stretch that DiMaggio had, he hit 15 home runs, 16 doubles, and drove in 55 runs.

Some important hitting records in the history of baseball include the lifetime record of 4,256 hits held by Pete Rose, the single season record of 232 walks held by Barry Bonds, and the career record of a batting average of.344 held by Ted Williams.

The single season with the greatest number of stolen bases

Vince Coleman now holds the record for the most bases stolen in a single season in college baseball. In 1983, while playing for Florida A&M, Coleman stole 139 bases, which puts him in possession of the record. Rickey Henderson now holds the record for most stolen bases in Major League Baseball (MLB). In 1982, while playing for the Oakland Athletics, Henderson stole 130 bases. It is generally agreed throughout baseball that Henderson was one of the best base stealers in the history of baseball, and it is quite doubtful that his record will be surpassed in the near future.

The lifetime record of 938 stolen bases held by Lou Brock, the single-season record of 123 stolen bases held by Tim Raines, and the career record of a batting average of.366 held by Ty Cobb are all important base stealing records in the annals of baseball history.

All-Time Marks for the Position of Manager

Over the years, baseball coaches have also established some outstanding records. Augie Garrido now holds the record for the most coaching victories in the history of collegiate baseball. Throughout the course of his career, he won 1,975 games as a head coach. Garrido is responsible for five different schools making it to the College World Series, and he has won the national championship with both Texas and Cal State Fullerton. Connie Mack now holds the record for the most coaching wins in the history of Major League Baseball (MLB). During his stint as the manager of the Philadelphia Athletics, Mack amassed a total of 3,731 victories. Mack oversaw the club during the first 50 seasons of its existence, during which time they won five World Series titles.

Other notable coaching records in the history of baseball include Tony La Russa's record of three World Series championships with three different teams, John McGraw's career record of 2,763 wins as a manager for the New York Giants, and Joe Torre's career record of 2,326 wins as a manager for the New York Yankees (the Oakland Athletics, St. Louis Cardinals, and Chicago White Sox).

Conclusion

Baseball is a sport that is steeped in history, and the records that have been established throughout the years by collegiate and Major League Baseball (MLB) players and coaches are a tribute to the game's illustrious history. These records highlight some of the most impressive accomplishments in the history of baseball, from Pete Incaviglia's record-setting season in college baseball to Joe DiMaggio's historic hitting streak in Major League Baseball, from Rickey Henderson's unparalleled ability to steal bases to Connie Mack's legendary career as a manager. It will be great to watch who players and coaches will stand up and smash these marks in the years to come as the game continues to progress and adapt.

Here are the top 50 MLB offensive records of all time:

1. Most career hits: Pete Rose, 4,256
2. Most career home runs: Barry Bonds, 762
3. Most career RBIs: Hank Aaron, 2,297
4. Highest career batting average (minimum 3,000 plate appearances): Ty Cobb, .366
5. Most career runs scored: Rickey Henderson, 2,295
6. Most career walks: Barry Bonds, 2,558
7. Most career strikeouts: Reggie Jackson, 2,597
8. Most career stolen bases: Rickey Henderson, 1,406

9. Most career total bases: Hank Aaron, 6,856

10. Most career doubles: Tris Speaker, 792

11. Most career triples: Sam Crawford, 309

12. Most career extra-base hits: Hank Aaron, 1,477

13. Most career grand slams: Alex Rodriguez, 25

14. Most home runs in a single season: Barry Bonds, 73

15. Most RBIs in a single season: Hack Wilson, 191

16. Highest batting average in a single season (minimum 502 plate appearances): Hugh Duffy, .440

17. Most runs scored in a single season: Babe Ruth, 177

18. Most total bases in a single season: Babe Ruth, 457

19. Most hits in a single season: Ichiro Suzuki, 262

20. Most doubles in a single season: Earl Webb, 67

21. Most triples in a single season: Chief Wilson, 36

22. Most extra-base hits in a single season: Babe Ruth, 119

23. Most consecutive games with a hit: Joe DiMaggio, 56

24. Most consecutive seasons with 100 or more runs scored: Babe Ruth, 13

25. Most consecutive seasons with 100 or more RBIs: Lou Gehrig, 13

26. Most consecutive seasons with 30 or more home runs: Barry Bonds, 12

27. Most consecutive seasons with 200 or more hits: Ichiro Suzuki, 10

28. Most seasons leading the league in batting average: Rogers Hornsby, 7

29. Most seasons leading the league in home runs: Babe Ruth, 12

30. Most seasons leading the league in RBIs: Hack Wilson, 4

31. Most seasons leading the league in runs scored: Babe Ruth, 8

32. Most seasons leading the league in stolen bases: Rickey Henderson, 12

33. Most seasons with 200 or more hits: Pete Rose, 10

34. Most seasons with 30 or more home runs: Babe Ruth, 11

35. Most seasons with 100 or more RBIs: Babe Ruth, 13

36. Most seasons with 100 or more runs scored: Babe Ruth, 13

37. Most seasons with 100 or more walks: Barry Bonds, 14

38. Most seasons with 50 or more stolen bases: Rickey Henderson, 10

39. Most seasons with a batting average of .400 or higher (minimum 400 plate appearances): Rogers Hornsby and Ty Cobb, 3

40. Most consecutive games with a home run: Ken Griffey Jr., 8

41. Most home runs in a single World Series: Reggie Jackson, 5

42. Most RBIs in a single World Series: Bobby Richardson, 12

43. Most hits in a single World Series: Marty Barrett, 13

44. Most doubles in a single World Series: Hank Bauer and Willie Stargell, 4

45. Most triples in a single World Series: Chief Wilson, 3

46. Most runs scored in a single World Series: Reggie Jackson, 10

47. Most total bases in a single World Series: Willie Stargell, 25

48. Most extra-base hits in a single World Series: Babe Ruth, 8

49. Most RBIs in a single game: Mark Whiten, 12

50. Most total bases in a single game: Shawn Green, 19

These records encompass a diverse selection of offensive statistics and highlight some of the most amazing individual performances in the annals of baseball's long and illustrious past. These records showcase the extraordinary talent and devotion of some of the best hitters the game has ever seen, from Pete Rose's lifetime hits record to Barry Bonds' career home runs record, from Hack Wilson's single-season RBI record to Ichiro Suzuki's single-season hits record.

Here are the top 50 MLB pitching records of all time:

1. Most career wins: Cy Young, 511

2. Most career strikeouts: Nolan Ryan, 5,714

3. Most career innings pitched: Cy Young, 7,356

4. Most career shutouts: Walter Johnson, 110

5. Most career complete games: Cy Young, 749

6. Most career no-hitters: Nolan Ryan, 7

7. Most strikeouts in a single season: Nolan Ryan, 383

8. Most consecutive strikeouts in a game: Tom Seaver, 10

9. Most strikeouts in a nine-inning game: Tom Cheney, 21

10. Most strikeouts in a postseason: Randy Johnson, 61

11. Lowest career ERA (minimum 1,000 innings pitched): Ed Walsh, 1.82

12. Most consecutive scoreless innings pitched: Orel Hershiser, 59

13. Most consecutive games started without a loss: Roger Clemens, 33

14. Most consecutive games won: Carl Hubbell, 24

15. Most consecutive complete games: Jack Taylor, 187

16. Most innings pitched in a single season: Old Hoss Radbourn, 678.2

17. Most wins in a single season: Jack Chesbro, 41

18. Most complete games in a single season: Will White, 75

19. Most shutouts in a single season: Grover Cleveland Alexander, 16

20. Most strikeouts in a single World Series game: Bob Gibson, 17

21. Most strikeouts in a single postseason: Curt Schilling, 56

22. Most saves in a single season: Francisco Rodriguez, 62

23. Most saves in a career: Mariano Rivera, 652

24. Most games finished in a single season: Francisco Rodriguez, 69

25. Most appearances in a single season: Mike Marshall, 106

26. Most wins in a season by a relief pitcher: John Smoltz, 24

27. Most strikeouts in a season by a relief pitcher: Dick Radatz, 181

28. Lowest ERA in a single season (minimum 162 innings pitched): Tim Keefe, 0.86

29. Most consecutive scoreless appearances: Orel Hershiser, 59

30. Most innings pitched in a postseason: Curt Schilling, 133.1

31. Most consecutive saves converted: Eric Gagne, 84

32. Most strikeouts per nine innings in a career (minimum 1,000 innings pitched): Randy Johnson, 10.61

33. Most consecutive starts without allowing a home run: Jake Arrieta, 24

34. Most innings pitched in a World Series: Christy Mathewson, 27

35. Most wins in a single postseason: Francisco Rodriguez, 5

36. Most saves in a single postseason: Koji Uehara, 7

37. Most games started in a career: Cy Young, 815

38. Most games pitched in a career: Jesse Orosco, 1,252

39. Most hits allowed in a career: Jamie Moyer, 4,714

40. Most earned runs allowed in a career: Nolan Ryan, 2,795

41. Most home runs allowed in a career: Jamie Moyer, 522

42. Most walks issued in a career: Nolan Ryan, 2,795

43. Most balks in a career: Steve Carlton, 90

44. Most wild pitches in a career: Phil Niekro, 290

45. Most hit batters in a career: Gus Weyhing, 277

46. Most games with at least 10 strikeouts in a season: Pedro Martinez, 23

47. Most seasons leading the league in strikeouts: Nolan Ryan, 11

48. Most seasons leading the league in ERA: Lefty Grove, 9

49. Most seasons leading the league in wins: Cy Young, 7

50. Most seasons leading the league in saves: Mariano Rivera, 5

These records showcase some of the finest pitching performances in the history of baseball, including Cy Young's record-setting career victories and Nolan Ryan's record for all-time strikeouts. Single-season records are also included on this list, such as Old Hoss Radbourn's astounding total of 678.2 innings pitched in a single season and Jack Chesbro's total of 41 victories in a single season. There are other records for bullpen pitchers, and Mariano Rivera holds both the single season record and the lifetime saves record. These records illustrate the extraordinary talent, stamina, and commitment that are necessary to achieve success as a pitcher in Major League Baseball.

Here are the top 50 MLB fielding records of all time:

1. Most career putouts by a first baseman: Jake Beckley, 23,711
2. Most career putouts by an outfielder: Tris Speaker, 6,038
3. Most career assists by a shortstop: Ozzie Smith, 8,375
4. Most career assists by a second baseman: Eddie Collins, 7,630
5. Most career assists by a third baseman: Brooks Robinson, 6,205
6. Most career double plays turned by a second baseman: Bill Maze-roski, 1,706
7. Most career double plays turned by a shortstop: Omar Vizquel, 1,734
8. Most career double plays turned by a third baseman: Brooks Robinson, 618
9. Most career total chances by a first baseman: Jake Beckley, 24,100
10. Most career total chances by a second baseman: Eddie Collins, 14,591
11. Most career total chances by a shortstop: Ozzie Smith, 14,955
12. Most career total chances by a third baseman: Brooks Robinson, 10,461
13. Highest career fielding percentage by a first baseman: Kevin Youkilis, .997

14. Highest career fielding percentage by a second baseman: Plácido Polanco, .993

15. Highest career fielding percentage by a shortstop: Omar Vizquel, .985

16. Highest career fielding percentage by a third baseman: Brooks Robinson, .971

17. Most consecutive errorless games by a second baseman: Plácido Polanco, 141

18. Most consecutive errorless games by a shortstop: Cal Ripken Jr., 95

19. Most consecutive errorless games by a third baseman: John Wehner, 99

20. Most Gold Glove awards won by a pitcher: Jim Kaat, 16

21. Most Gold Glove awards won by a catcher: Ivan Rodriguez, 13

22. Most Gold Glove awards won by a first baseman: Keith Hernandez, 11

23. Most Gold Glove awards won by a second baseman: Roberto Alomar, 10

24. Most Gold Glove awards won by a third baseman: Brooks Robinson, 16

25. Most Gold Glove awards won by a shortstop: Ozzie Smith, 13

26. Most Gold Glove awards won by an outfielder: Willie Mays, 12

27. Most consecutive Gold Glove awards won by a pitcher: Greg Maddux, 18

28. Most consecutive Gold Glove awards won by a catcher: Ivan Rodriguez, 10

29. Most consecutive Gold Glove awards won by a first baseman: Keith Hernandez, 6

30. Most consecutive Gold Glove awards won by a second baseman: Roberto Alomar, 10

31. Most consecutive Gold Glove awards won by a third baseman: Scott Rolen, 8

32. Most consecutive Gold Glove awards won by a shortstop: Ozzie Smith, 13

33. Most consecutive Gold Glove awards won by an outfielder: Ichiro Suzuki, 10

34. Most assists in a season by a first baseman: Charlie Grimm, 485

35. Most assists in a season by a second baseman: Charlie Gehringer, 628

36. Most assists in a season by a shortstop: Honus Wagner, 748

37. Most assists in a season by a third baseman: Pie Traynor, 549

38. Most putouts in a season by a first baseman: Jake Daub

39Most putouts in a season by a second baseman: Nap Lajoie, 512

38. Most putouts in a season by a shortstop: George McBride, 454

39. Most putouts in a season by a third baseman: Brooks Robinson, 154

40. Most double plays turned in a season by a first baseman: Mark Grace, 174

41. Most double plays turned in a season by a second baseman: Bill Mazeroski, 161

42. Most double plays turned in a season by a shortstop: Ozzie Smith, 114

43. Most double plays turned in a season by a third baseman: Brooks Robinson, 44

44. Most consecutive errorless games by a first baseman: Kevin Youkilis, 238

45. Most consecutive errorless games by an outfielder: Darren Lewis, 392

46. Most assists in a game by a first baseman: Jake Beckley, 23

47. Most double plays turned in a game by a team: Detroit Tigers, 7

48. Most innings played without an error by a team: Boston Red Sox, 20,984.2

These statistics highlight some of the most impressive defensive plays in the annals of baseball's long and illustrious history. These demonstrate the amazing range, accuracy, and agility that is necessary to perform defensively, ranging from Jake Beckley's record-setting career putouts at first base to Bill Mazeroski's double-play turning skills at second base. Gold Glove awards are also presented, and among the most decorated defenders of all time are Keith Hernandez, Roberto Alomar, and Brooks Robinson. The inclusion of records for consecutive errorless games and errorless innings played by individuals and teams demonstrates the significance of maintaining consistency and relying on one's abilities when fielding the ball.

Here are the TOP 50 at the NCAA College Level. The top 50 NCAA college baseball offensive records would be too lengthy for a single response. However, I can provide you with a list of the players and their respective records:

1. Phil Stephenson – Wichita State- most career hits
2. Kellen Winslow - Missouri- most career home runs
3. Pete Incaviglia -Oklahoma State- most career RBIs
4. Robin Ventura -Oklahoma State- most career runs scored.
5. Desmond Cambridge of Alabama A&M- most career stolen bases
6. Phil Stephenson - Wichita State- most hits in a season and most career doubles
7. Pete Incaviglia – Oklahoma State-most home runs in a season and most total bases in a season.
8. Pete Incaviglia -Oklahoma State- most RBIs in a season
9. Dave Magadan -Alabama- most runs scored in a season and highest career batting average.
10. Vince Coleman -Florida A&M- most stolen bases in a season and most consecutive games with a stolen base

11. Dave Magadan -Alabama- highest career batting average

12. Tim Wallach -Cal State Fullerton- most hits in a single game

13. Brad Wilkerson -Florida- most home runs in a single game.

14. Eric Chavez - most RBIs in a single game

15. John Powell -Western Carolina- most runs scored in a single game.

16. Mike Lansing -Wichita State- most stolen bases in a single game

17. Damian Costantino -Salve Regina University- most consecutive games with a hit

18. Bill Goldsworthy -Minnesota- most consecutive games with a home run and most consecutive games with a run scored.

19. Robin Ventura – Oklahoma State-most consecutive games with an RBI

20. Vince Coleman -Florida A&M- most consecutive games with a stolen base

21. Phil Stephenson -Wichita State- most career triples

22. Jim Greengrass – Pacific University-most doubles in a season

23. Jeff Heathcock – Mississippi State-most career triples

24. Pat Burrell -Miami- most triples in a season

25. Bill Bordley -Stanford- most walks in a season and most consecutive games with a walk in a conference

26. Pete Incaviglia -Oklahoma State- most career total bases and most career intentional walks

27. Pete Incaviglia -Oklahoma State- most total bases in a season and most intentional walks in a season

28. John Fishell -Cal State Fullerton most career at-bats

29. Jon Zuber -Texas Tech- most at-bats in a season

30. Tim Raley -Mount Olive College- most games played in a career.

31. Brian Kelley -Arizona State- most games played in a season

32. Marc Bragdon -USC- most career sacrifice hits

33. Gary Hatch – Brigham Young-most sacrifice hits in a season

34. Tom Sergio -Creighton University- most career sacrifice flies

35. Matt Smith -Eastern Michigan- most sacrifice flies in a season

36. John Fishel -Cal State Fullerton- most career hit by pitches.

37. Kevin Youkilis – Cincinnati-most hit by pitches in a season

38. Pete Incaviglia – Oklahoma State-most career intentional walks

39. Pete Incaviglia -Oklahoma State- most intentional walks in a season

40. Dan Dement -Illinois- most consecutive games played.

41. Bill Hasselman -San Jose State- most consecutive games started.

42. Damian Costantino -Salve Regina University- most consecutive games with a hit in a conference and most consecutive games with a hit in a season

43. Bill Goldsworthy -Minnesota- most consecutive games with a run scored in a conference and most consecutive games with a run scored in a season.

44. Bill Bordley -Stanford- most consecutive games with a walk in a conference

45. Ryan Jackson – Miami-most consecutive games with a hit

46. Keith Moreland -Texas University- most consecutive games with a hit in a season

47. Josh Harrison -Cincinnati- most consecutive games with a run scored.

48. Jerrey Thurston -Brigham Young- most consecutive games with a stolen base in a season

49. Daniel Nava -Santa Clara- most consecutive games with a walk

50. Aaron Holbert -Oral Roberts- most consecutive games with a hit by pitch

Top NCAA Pitching Records of all time.

Here are the top 50 NCAA pitching records of all time:

1. Most career wins: Paul Petrino, 54
2. Most career strikeouts: Justin Verlander, 479
3. Most career innings pitched: Kyle Peterson, 504.0
4. Most career complete games: Kyle Peterson, 36
5. Most career shutouts: Joe Magrane, 15
6. Most consecutive innings pitched without allowing an earned run: Kris Benson, 47.1
7. Most strikeouts in a season: David Cone, 198
8. Most strikeouts per nine innings in a season (minimum 50 innings pitched): Stephen Strasburg, 17.7
9. Most strikeouts in a game: Kerry Wood, 20
10. Most innings pitched in a game: Neal Heaton and Mark Wohlers, 18.0
11. Most complete games in a season: Kyle Peterson, 14
12. Most shutouts in a season: Bob Horner and Steve Arlin, 7
13. Most wins in a season: Bill Bordley and Mike Loynd, 20
14. Most saves in a season: Tyler Rogers, 24
15. Most strikeouts in a College World Series: Ron Polk, 56
16. Most innings pitched in a College World Series: Eddie Bane, 27.0
17. Most strikeouts in a season by a relief pitcher: Todd Belitz, 161
18. Most wins in a career by a relief pitcher: Ryan Doherty, 34
19. Most saves in a career: Huston Street, 41
20. Most games pitched in a career: Jason Windsor, 97
21. Most consecutive scoreless innings pitched: John McDonald, 73.1

22. Most consecutive games won: Steve Arlin, 16

23. Most consecutive complete games: Marty Clary, 16

24. Most consecutive shutouts: Mark Prior, 4

25. Most consecutive innings without allowing a run: Ben McDonald, 44.2

26. Most consecutive innings without allowing a hit: Bob Porterfield, 27.0

27. Lowest career ERA (minimum 250 innings pitched): Mark Appel, 2.14

28. Lowest single-season ERA (minimum 50 innings pitched): Tim Lincecum, 1.94

29. Most shutouts in a single NCAA Tournament: Jim Abbott, 3

30. Most wins in a single NCAA Tournament: Greg Swindell, 5

31. Most strikeouts in a single NCAA Tournament: Darren Dreifort, 48

32. Most innings pitched in a single NCAA Tournament: Rick Austin and Brad Brach, 30.0

33. Most consecutive scoreless innings pitched in a College World Series: Bob Gibson, 22.0

34. Most strikeouts in a season by a freshman: Stephen Strasburg, 133

35. Most strikeouts in a season by a sophomore: Mark Prior, 202

36. Most strikeouts in a season by a junior: Justin Verlander, 151

37. Most strikeouts in a season by a senior: David Cone, 198

38. Most strikeouts in a career by a freshman: Mark Prior, 163

39. Most strikeouts in a career by a sophomore: Justin Verlander, 427

40. Most strikeouts in a career by a junior: David Cone, 343

41. Most strikeouts in a career by a senior: Jim Abbott, 361

42. Most wins in a career by a freshman: John Burke, 19

43. Most wins in a career by a sophomore: Jerry Don Gleaton,

44. Most wins in a career by a junior: Justin Simmons, 44

45. Most wins in a career by a senior: Bill Bordley, 45

46. Most saves in a season by a freshman: Tyler Johnson, 17

47. Most saves in a season by a sophomore: J.B. Wendelken, 16

48. Most saves in a season by a junior: Jack Armstrong Jr. and Todd Belitz, 19

49. Most saves in a season by a senior: Tony Zych, 17

50. Most saves in a career by a freshman: J.B. Wendelken, 25

Here are the colleges that the athletes from the top 50 NCAA pitching records played for:

1. Paul Petrino - Oral Roberts University

2. Justin Verlander - Old Dominion University

3. Kyle Peterson - Stanford University

4. Joe Magrane - University of Arizona

5. Kris Benson - Clemson University

6. David Cone - University of Missouri

7. Stephen Strasburg - San Diego State University

8. Kerry Wood - Grand Prairie High School (TX)

9. Neal Heaton - University of Miami

10. Mark Wohlers - University of Georgia

11. Bob Horner - Arizona State University

12. Steve Arlin - Ohio State University

13. Bill Bordley - Stanford University

14. Mike Loynd - Florida State University

15. Tyler Rogers - Austin Peay State University

16. Ron Polk - Mississippi State University

17. Eddie Bane - Arizona State University

18. Todd Belitz - University of New Orleans

19. Ryan Doherty - University of Notre Dame

20. Huston Street - University of Texas at Austin

21. Jason Windsor - California State University, Fullerton

22. John McDonald - Pepperdine University

23. Steve Arlin - Ohio State University

24. Marty Clary - Pepperdine University

25. Mark Prior - University of Southern California

26. Ben McDonald - Louisiana State University

27. Bob Porterfield - High Point University

28. Mark Appel - Stanford University

29. Tim Lincecum - University of Washington

30. Jim Abbott - University of Michigan

31. Greg Swindell - University of Texas at Austin

32. Darren Dreifort - Wichita State University

33. Rick Austin - California State University, Fullerton

34. Brad Brach - Monmouth University

35. Bob Gibson - Creighton University

36. John Burke - University of Florida

37. Jerry Don Gleaton - Texas Christian University

38. Justin Simmons - University of California, Irvine

39. Bill Bordley - Stanford University

40. Tyler Johnson - Stony Brook University

41. J.B. Wendelken - Middle Georgia State University

42. Jack Armstrong Jr. - Vanderbilt University

43. Todd Belitz - University of New Orleans

44. Tony Zych - University of Louisville

45. J.B. Wendelken - Middle Georgia State University

46. Seth Greisinger - University of Virginia

47. Brett Sinkbeil - Missouri State University

48. Scott Bittle - University of Mississippi

49. Drew Smyly - University of Arkansas

50. Mike Mayers - University of Mississippi

Note: Some of the pitchers played for multiple schools during their college career, but the schools listed above are where they played the majority of their college games.

These records are a testament to the extraordinary skill and unwavering commitment of some of the most accomplished pitchers in NCAA history. These statistics highlight the stamina and talent necessary to be a successful collegiate pitcher, from Paul Petrino's record for career wins to Kyle Peterson's record for career innings pitched and complete games. In this list are also single-season records, like Stephen Strasburg's remarkable 17.7 strikeouts per nine innings and David Cone's incredible 198 strikeouts in a single season. Records for relief pitchers are also featured, with Huston Street owning the record for the most saves in a career and Tyler Johnson holding the record for the most saves in a single season by a freshman. The huge influence that pitchers can have on the game and the significance of great pitching in college baseball are both illustrated by these records.

CHAPTER FIVE

Baseball Trivia

Baseball is a sport that has been enjoyed for over a century, with a rich history and tradition that has captivated fans worldwide. In this chapter, we will explore some fascinating baseball trivia, including the highest paid player in MLB history, the first team to play in the World Series, the oldest stadium in Major League Baseball, and the significance of the seventh inning stretch.

1. Who is the highest-paid player in MLB history?
2. Which player has won the most MVP awards in MLB history?
3. Who was the first African-American player to play in Major League Baseball?
4. Who is the only player to hit two grand slams in one inning?
5. Which pitcher has the most strikeouts in a single season?
6. Who holds the record for the most home runs in a single season?
7. Who is the only player to have won the batting title in each league?
8. Who was the first player to hit 50 home runs in a season?
9. Which player has the most career stolen bases?
10. Who is the only pitcher to have won the MVP award twice?

11. Which team holds the record for the most World Series championships?

12. Who holds the record for the most hits in a single season?

13. Who was the first player to hit 500 home runs?

14. Who holds the record for the most consecutive games with a hit?

15. Which pitcher has the most career wins?

16. Who was the first player to win the Triple Crown in MLB history?

17. Who holds the record for the most RBIs in a single season?

18. Who is the only player to hit a home run in his first Major League at-bat in a World Series game?

19. Which team won the first World Series?

20. Who holds the record for the most saves in a single season?

21. Who was the first player to steal 100 bases in a season?

22. Which pitcher has the most no-hitters in MLB history?

23. Who is the only player to have hit for the cycle twice in the same season?

24. Who was the first player to hit a home run in an All-Star Game?

25. Which pitcher has the most career strikeouts?

26. Who holds the record for the most hits in a career?

27. Who was the first player to hit 60 home runs in a season?

28. Which team has the longest World Series drought?

29. Who is the only player to have won the MVP award unanimously?

30. Who holds the record for the most consecutive scoreless innings pitched in the World Series?

31. Who was the first player to hit a home run at Yankee Stadium?

32. Which pitcher has the most complete games in a single season?

33. Who holds the record for the most consecutive games played?

34. Who was the first player to win the Cy Young Award?

35. Who holds the record for the most walks in a single season?

36. Who is the only pitcher to have won the Cy Young Award in both leagues?

37. Who was the first player to hit a home run in a regular-season game outside of North America?

38. Which team has the most losses in MLB history?

39. Who holds the record for the most stolen bases in a single season?

40. Who was the first player to hit four home runs in a game?

41. Who holds the record for the most strikeouts in a single game?

42. Who is the only player to have won the World Series MVP award with two different teams?

43. Who was the first player to win the Gold Glove award?

44. Who holds the record for the most Gold Glove awards in MLB history?

45. Which team has the most wins in a single season?

46. Who was the first player to win the Silver Slugger award?

47. Who holds the record for the most Silver Slugger awards in MLB history?

48. Which pitcher has the lowest career ERA in MLB history?

49. Who was the first player to hit a home run in a Major League game played outside of the United States?

50. Who holds the record for the most consecutive games with a home run?

51. Who is the only player to have won the Rookie of the Year award unanimously?

52. Who holds the record for the most saves in a career?

53. Which team has the most losses in a single season?

54. Who was the first player to hit a home run in an MLB game played in Japan?

55. Who holds the record for the most RBIs in a career?

56. Which pitcher has the most career shutouts?

57. Who was the first player to hit a walk-off home run in a World Series game?

58. Who holds the record for the most triples in a single season?

59. Who is the only pitcher to have won the MVP award in a losing season?

60. Who holds the record for the most stolen bases in a career?

61. Which team has the most consecutive losses in MLB history?

62. Who was the first player to hit a home run in an MLB game played in Europe?

63. Who holds the record for the most strikeouts in a career?

64. Who is the only player to have won the MVP award in his final season?

65. Which pitcher has the most career wins without ever winning a Cy Young Award?

66. Who was the first player to hit a home run in an MLB game played in Mexico?

67. Who holds the record for the most doubles in a single season?

68. Who is the only pitcher to have won the World Series MVP award in a losing effort?

69. Who holds the record for the most hits in a single game?

70. Who was the first player to hit a home run in an MLB game played in Australia?

71. Which pitcher has the most complete games in MLB history?

72. Who holds the record for the most RBIs in a single game?

73. Who is the only player to have won the MVP award in a World Series that his team lost?

74. Who holds the record for the most sacrifice bunts in a career?

75. Who was the first player to hit a home run in an MLB game played in Puerto Rico?

76. Which team has the longest winning streak in MLB history?

77. Who holds the record for the most hits in a single World Series?

78. Who is the only player to have won the Cy Young Award in three consecutive seasons?

79. Who holds the record for the most sacrifice flies in a career?

80. Who was the first player to hit a home run in an MLB game played in China?

81. Which pitcher has the most career losses?

82. Who holds the record for the most RBIs in a World Series?

83. Who is the only player to have hit three home runs in a single World Series game twice?

84. Who holds the record for the most times being hit by a pitch in a career?

85. Who was the first player to hit a home run in an MLB game played in the Dominican Republic?

86. Which team has the most wins in MLB history?

87. Who holds the record for the most doubles in a career?

88. Who is the only player to have hit two walk-off home runs in a single World Series?

89. Who holds the record for the most runs scored in a single season?

90. Who was the first player to hit a home run in an MLB game played in Panama?

91. Which pitcher has the most career strikeouts per nine innings pitched? 92. Who holds the record for the most walks in a career?

93. Who is the only player to have hit a home run into the upper deck at Yankee Stadium, Tiger Stadium, and Fenway Park?

94. Who holds the record for the most strikeouts in a single World Series?

95. Who was the first player to hit a home run in an MLB game played in South Korea?

96. Which team has the most losses in World Series history?

97. Who holds the record for the most extra-base hits in a single season?

98. Who is the only player to have hit two grand slams in a single inning in a Minor League Baseball game?

99. Who holds the record for the most innings pitched in a single season?

100. Who was the first player to hit a home run in an MLB game played in Taiwan?

Now that we've explored some fascinating baseball trivia, let's take a closer look at some of the topics we've covered.

The highest paid player in MLB history: The highest-paid player in MLB history is Mike Trout, who signed a 12-year, $426.5 million contract with the Los Angeles Angels in 2019. Other players who have earned significant amounts of money in their careers include Alex Rodriguez, Derek Jeter, and Clayton Kershaw.

The first team to play in the World Series: The first World Series was played in 1903 between the Pittsburgh Pirates and the Boston Americans (now the Red Sox). The series has since evolved to include more teams and has become one of the most exciting events in sports.

The oldest stadium in Major League Baseball: The oldest stadium still in use in Major League Baseball is Fenway Park, which opened in 1912 and is the home of the Boston Red Sox. The stadium is significant to the game because of its unique features, including the Green Monster and the manual scoreboard.

The significance of the seventh-inning stretch: The tradition of the seventh-inning stretch is believed to have started in 1910 during a game between the New York Giants and the Chicago Cubs. The origins of the tradition are uncertain, but it is now a staple of baseball games, with fans standing up and stretching during the seventh-inning break.

In conclusion, baseball is a sport with a rich history and tradition that has captured the hearts of fans for over a century. Whether you're a diehard fan or a casual observer, the trivia and history surrounding the game are fascinating and worth exploring.

Trivia Answers

Here are the answers to the baseball trivia questions:

1. Who is the highest-paid player in MLB history? Mike Trout
2. Which player has won the most MVP awards in MLB history? Barry Bonds
3. Who was the first African American player to play in Major League Baseball? Jackie Robinson
4. Who is the only player to hit two grand slams in one inning? Fernando Tatis Sr.
5. Which pitcher has the most strikeouts in a single season? Nolan Ryan
6. Who holds the record for the most home runs in a single season? Barry Bonds
7. Who is the only player to have won the batting title in each league? Ed Delahanty
8. Who was the first player to hit 50 home runs in a season? Babe Ruth
9. Which player has the most career stolen bases? Rickey Henderson
10. Who is the only pitcher to have won the MVP award twice? Roger Clemens

11. Which team holds the record for the most World Series championships? New York Yankees

12. Who holds the record for the most hits in a single season? Ichiro Suzuki

13. Who was the first player to hit 500 home runs? Babe Ruth

14. Who holds the record for the most consecutive games with a hit? Joe DiMaggio

15. Which pitcher has the most career wins? Cy Young

16. Who was the first player to win the Triple Crown in MLB history? Hugh Duffy

17. Who holds the record for the most RBIs in a single season? Hack Wilson

18. Who is the only player to hit a home run in his first Major League at-bat in a World Series game? Mickey Mantle

19. Which team won the first World Series? Boston Americans (now the Red Sox)

20. Who holds the record for the most saves in a single season? Francisco Rodriguez

21. Who was the first player to steal 100 bases in a season? Rickey Henderson

22. Which pitcher has the most no-hitters in MLB history? Nolan Ryan

23. Who is the only player to have hit for the cycle twice in the same season? Babe Herman

24. Who was the first player to hit a home run in an All-Star Game? Ted Williams

25. Which pitcher has the most career strikeouts? Nolan Ryan

26. Who holds the record for the most hits in a career? Pete Rose

27. Who was the first player to hit 60 home runs in a season? Babe Ruth

28. Which team has the longest World Series drought? Cleveland Indians (last won in 1948)

29. Who is the only player to have won the MVP award unanimously? Bryce Harper

30. Who holds the record for the most consecutive scoreless innings pitched in the World Series? Christy Mathewson

31. Who was the first player to hit a home run at Yankee Stadium? Babe Ruth

32. Which pitcher has the most complete games in a single season? Jack Chesbro

33. Who holds the record for the most consecutive games played? Cal Ripken Jr.

34. Who was the first player to win the Cy Young Award? Don Newcombe

35. Who holds the record for the most walks in a single season? Barry Bonds

36. Who is the only pitcher to have won the Cy Young Award in both leagues? Roger Clemens

37. Who was the first player to hit a home run in a regular-season game outside of North America? George Bell

38. Which team has the most losses in MLB history? Philadelphia Phillies

39. Who holds the record for the most stolen bases in a single season? Rickey Henderson

40. Who was the first player to hit four home runs in a game? Bobby Lowe

41. Who holds the record for the most strikeouts in a single game? Tom Cheney

42. Who is the only player to have won the World Series MVP award with two different teams? Frank Robinson

43. Who was the first player to win the Gold Glove award? Don Drysdale

44. Who holds the record for the most Gold Glove awards in MLB history? Greg Maddux

45. Which team has the most wins in a single season? Seattle Mariners (116 wins in 2001)

46. Who was the first player to win the Silver Slugger award? Mike Schmidt

47. Who holds the record for the most Silver Slugger awards in MLB history? Barry Bonds

48. Which pitcher has the lowest career ERA in MLB history? Addie Joss

49. Who was the first player to hit a home run in a Major League game played outside of the United States? Rusty Staub

50. Who holds the record for the most consecutive games with a home run? Ken Griffey Jr.

51. Who is the only player to have won the Rookie of the Year award unanimously? Derek Jeter

52. Who holds the record for the most saves in a career? Mariano Rivera

53. Which team has the most losses in a single season? Detroit Tigers (119 losses in 2003)

54. Who was the first player to hit a home run in an MLB game played in Japan? Alfonso Soriano

55. Who holds the record for the most RBIs in a career? Hank Aaron

56. Which pitcher has the most career shutouts? Walter Johnson

57. Who was the first player to hit a walk-off home run in a World Series game? Bill Mazeroski

58. Who holds the record for the most triples in a single season? Chief Wilson

59. Who is the only pitcher to have won the MVP award in a losing season? Vida Blue

60. Who holds the record for the most stolen bases in a career? Rickey Henderson

61. Which team has the most consecutive losses in MLB history? Cleveland Indians (22 losses in 2017)

62. Who was the first player to hit a home run in an MLB game played in Europe? David Ortiz

63. Who holds the record for the most strikeouts in a career? Nolan Ryan

64. Who is the only player to have won the MVP award in his final season? David Ortiz

65. Which pitcher has the most career wins without ever winning a Cy Young Award? Tom Glavine

66. Who was the first player to hit a home run in an MLB game played in Mexico? Dusty Baker

67. Who holds the record for the most doubles in a single season? Earl Webb

68. Who is the only pitcher to have won the World Series MVP award in a losing effort? Bobby Richardson

69. Who holds the record for the most hits in a single game? Wilbert Robinson

70. Who was the first player to hit a home run in an MLB game played in Australia? Paul Goldschmidt

71. Which pitcher has the most complete games in MLB history? Cy Young

72. Who holds the record for the most RBIs in a single game? Mark Whiten

73. Who is the only player to have won the MVP award in a World Series that his team lost? Bobby Richardson

74. Who holds the record for the most sacrifice bunts in a career? Eddie Collins

75. Who was the first player to hit a home run in an MLB game played in Puerto Rico? Roberto Clemente

76. Which team has the longest winning streak in MLB history? Cleveland Indians (22 games in 2017)

77. Who holds the record for the most hits in a single World Series? Bobby Richardson

78. Who is the only player to have won the Cy Young Award in three consecutive seasons? Greg Maddux

79. Who holds the record for the most sacrifice flies in a career? Eddie Murray

80. Who was the first player to hit a home run in an MLB game played in China? Ryan Spilborghs

81. Which pitcher has the most career losses? Cy Young

82. Who holds the record for the most RBIs in a World Series? Bobby Richardson

83. Who is the only player to have hit three home runs in a single World Series game twice? Babe Ruth

84. Who holds the record for the most times being hit by a pitch in a career? Hughie Jennings

85. Who was the first player to hit a home run in an MLB game played in the Dominican Republic? George Bell

86. Which team has the most wins in MLB history? New York Yankees

87. Who holds the record for the most doubles in a career? Tris Speaker

88. Who is the only player to have hit two walk-off home runs in a single World Series? Babe Ruth

89. Who holds the record for the most runs scored in a single season? Babe Ruth

90. Who was the first player to hit a home run in an MLB game played in Panama? Luis Alicea

91. Which pitcher has the most career strikeouts per nine innings pitched? Randy Johnson

92. Who holds the record for the most walks in a career? Barry Bonds

93. Who is the only player to have hit a home run into the upper deck at Yankee Stadium, Tiger Stadium, and Fenway Park? Mickey Mantle

94. Who holds the record for the most strikeouts in a single World Series? Bob Gibson

95. Who was the first player to hit a home run in an MLB game played in South Korea? Ryan Langerhans

96. Which team has the most losses in World Series history? New York Yankees

97. Who holds the record for the most extra-base hits in a single season? Barry Bonds

98. Who is the only player to have hit two grand slams in a single inning in a Minor League Baseball game? Tuffy Rhodes

99. Who holds the record for the most innings pitched in a single season? Old Hoss Radbourn

100. Who was the first player to hit a home run in an MLB game played in Taiwan? Kirk Gibson

Here is a list of every MLB World Series champion, including the team, manager, and Series MVP, from the first World Series in 1903 to the most recent in 2022:

1903 - Boston Americans (now Red Sox), Manager: Jimmy Collins, Series MVP: None

1904 - No World Series played due to a dispute between the National and American Leagues

1905 - New York Giants, Manager: John McGraw, Series MVP: None

1906 - Chicago White Sox, Manager: Fielder Jones, Series MVP: None

1907 - Chicago Cubs, Manager: Frank Chance, Series MVP: None

1908 - Chicago Cubs, Manager: Frank Chance, Series MVP: None

1909 - Pittsburgh Pirates, Manager: Fred Clarke, Series MVP: None

1910 - Philadelphia Athletics, Manager: Connie Mack, Series MVP: None

1911 - Philadelphia Athletics, Manager: Connie Mack, Series MVP: None

1912 - Boston Red Sox, Manager: Jake Stahl, Series MVP: None

1913 - Philadelphia Athletics, Manager: Connie Mack, Series MVP: None

1914 - Boston Braves (now Atlanta Braves), Manager: George Stallings, Series MVP: None

1915 - Boston Red Sox, Manager: Bill Carrigan, Series MVP: None

1916 - Boston Red Sox, Manager: Bill Carrigan, Series MVP: None

1917 - Chicago White Sox, Manager: Pants Rowland, Series MVP: Eddie Cicotte

1918 - Boston Red Sox, Manager: Ed Barrow, Series MVP: None

1919 - Cincinnati Reds, Manager: Pat Moran, Series MVP: None

1920 - Cleveland Indians, Manager: Tris Speaker, Series MVP: None

1921 - New York Giants, Manager: John McGraw, Series MVP: None

1922 - New York Giants, Manager: John McGraw, Series MVP: None

1923 - New York Yankees, Manager: Miller Huggins, Series MVP: None

1924 - Washington Senators (now Minnesota Twins), Manager: Bucky Harris, Series MVP: None

1925 - Pittsburgh Pirates, Manager: Bill McKechnie, Series MVP: None

1926 - St. Louis Cardinals, Manager: Rogers Hornsby, Series MVP: None

1927 - New York Yankees, Manager: Miller Huggins, Series MVP: None

1928 - New York Yankees, Manager: Miller Huggins, Series MVP: None

1929 - Philadelphia Athletics, Manager: Connie Mack, Series MVP: None

1930 - Philadelphia Athletics, Manager: Connie Mack, Series MVP: None

1931 - St. Louis Cardinals, Manager: Gabby Street, Series MVP: None

1932 - New York Yankees, Manager: Joe McCarthy, Series MVP: None

1933 - New York Giants, Manager: Bill Terry, Series MVP: None

1934 - St. Louis Cardinals, Manager: Frankie Frisch, Series MVP: Dizzy Dean

1935 - Detroit Tigers, Manager: Mickey Cochrane, Series MVP: None

1936 - New York Yankees, Manager: Joe McCarthy, Series MVP: Tony Lazzeri

1937 - New York Yankees, Manager: Joe McCarthy, Series MVP: Charlie Keller

1938 - New York Yankees, Manager: Joe McCarthy, Series MVP: Lefty Gomez

1939 - New York Yankees, Manager: Joe McCarthy, Series MVP: Joe Gordon

1940 - Cincinnati Reds, Manager: Bill McKechnie, Series MVP: None

1941 - New York Yankees, Manager: Joe McCarthy, Series MVP: Phil Rizzuto

1942 - St. Louis Cardinals, Manager: Billy Southworth, Series MVP: Mort Cooper

1943 - New York Yankees, Manager: Joe McCarthy, Series MVP: Spud Chandler

1944 - St. Louis Cardinals, Manager: Billy Southworth, Series MVP: Marty Marion

1945 - Detroit Tigers, Manager: Steve O'Neill, Series MVP: Hal Newhouser

1946 - St. Louis Cardinals, Manager: Eddie Dyer, Series MVP: Enos Slaughter

1947 - New York Yankees, Manager: Bucky Harris, Series MVP: Phil Rizzuto

1948 - Cleveland Indians, Manager: Lou Boudreau, Series MVP: Larry Doby

1949 - New York Yankees, Manager: Casey Stengel, Series MVP: Joe DiMaggio

1950 - New York Yankees, Manager: Casey Stengel, Series MVP: Phil Rizzuto

1951 - New York Yankees, Manager: Casey Stengel, Series MVP: None

1952 - New York Yankees, Manager: Casey Stengel, Series MVP: Johnny Mize

1953 - New York Yankees, Manager: Casey Stengel, Series MVP: Billy Martin

1954 - New York Giants, Manager: Leo Durocher, Series MVP: Willie Mays

1955 - Brooklyn Dodgers, Manager: Walter Alston, Series MVP: Johnny Podres

1956 - New York Yankees, Manager: Casey Stengel, Series MVP: Don Larsen

1957 - Milwaukee Braves (now Atlanta Braves), Manager: Fred Haney, Series MVP: Lew Burdette

1958 - New York Yankees, Manager: Casey Stengel, Series MVP: Bob Turley

1959 - Los Angeles Dodgers, Manager: Walter Alston, Series MVP: Larry Sherry

1960 - Pittsburgh Pirates, Manager: Danny Murtaugh, Series MVP: Bobby Richardson

1961 - New York Yankees, Manager: Ralph Houk, Series MVP: Whitey Ford

1962 - New York Yankees, Manager: Ralph Houk, Series MVP: Ralph Terry

1963 - Los Angeles Dodgers, Manager: Walter Alston, Series MVP: Sandy Koufax

1964 - St. Louis Cardinals, Manager: Johnny Keane, Series MVP: Bob Gibson

1965 - Los Angeles Dodgers, Manager: Walter Alston, Series MVP: Sandy Koufax

1966 - Baltimore Orioles, Manager: Hank Bauer, Series MVP: Frank Robinson

1967 - St. Louis Cardinals, Manager: Red Schoendienst, Series MVP: Bob Gibson

1968 - Detroit Tigers, Manager: Mayo Smith, Series MVP: Mickey Lolich

1969 - New York Mets, Manager: Gil Hodges, Series MVP: Donn Clendenon

1970 - Baltimore Orioles, Manager: Earl Weaver, Series MVP: Brooks Robinson

1971 - Pittsburgh Pirates, Manager: Danny Murtaugh, Series MVP: Roberto Clemente

1972 - Oakland Athletics, Manager: Dick Williams, Series MVP: Gene Tenace

1973 - Oakland Athletics, Manager: Dick Williams, Series MVP: Reggie Jackson

1974 - Oakland Athletics, Manager: Alvin Dark, Series MVP: Rollie Fingers

1975 - Cincinnati Reds, Manager: Sparky Anderson, Series MVP: Pete Rose

1976 - Cincinnati Reds, Manager: Sparky Anderson, Series MVP: Johnny Bench

1977 - New York Yankees, Manager: Billy Martin, Series MVP: Reggie Jackson

1978 - New York Yankees, Manager: Bob Lemon, Series MVP: Bucky Dent

1979 - Pittsburgh Pirates, Manager: Chuck Tanner, Series MVP: Willie Stargell

1980 - Philadelphia Phillies, Manager: Dallas Green, Series MVP: Mike Schmidt

1981 - Los Angeles Dodgers, Manager: Tommy Lasorda, Series MVP: Ron Cey, Pedro Guerrero, and Steve Yeager (co-MVPs)

1982 - St. Louis Cardinals, Manager: Whitey Herzog, Series MVP: Darrell Porter

1983 - Baltimore Orioles, Manager: Joe Altobelli, Series MVP: Rick Dempsey

1984 - Detroit Tigers, Manager: Sparky Anderson, Series MVP: Alan Trammell

1985 - Kansas City Royals, Manager: Dick Howser, Series MVP: Bret Saberhagen

1986 - New York Mets, Manager: Davey Johnson, Series MVP: Ray Knight

1987 - Minnesota Twins, Manager: Tom Kelly, Series MVP: Frank Viola

1988 - Los Angeles Dodgers, Manager: Tommy Lasorda, Series MVP: Orel Hershiser

1989 - Oakland Athletics, Manager: Tony La Russa, Series MVP: Dave Stewart

1990 - Cincinnati Reds, Manager: Lou Piniella, Series MVP: Jose Rijo

1991 - Minnesota Twins, Manager: Tom Kelly, Series MVP: Jack Morris

1992 - Toronto Blue Jays, Manager: Cito Gaston, Series MVP: Pat Borders

1993 - Toronto Blue Jays, Manager: Cito Gaston, Series MVP: Paul Molitor

1994 - No World Series played due to a players' strike

1995 - Atlanta Braves, Manager: Bobby Cox, Series MVP: Tom Glavine

1996 - New York Yankees, Manager: Joe Torre, Series MVP: John Wetteland

1997 - Florida Marlins, Manager: Jim Leyland, Series MVP: Livan Hernandez

1998 - New York Yankees, Manager: Joe Torre, Series MVP: Scott Brosius

1999 - New York Yankees, Manager: Joe Torre, Series MVP: Mariano Rivera

2000 - New York Yankees, Manager: Joe Torre, Series MVP: Derek Jeter

2001 - Arizona Diamondbacks, Manager: Bob Brenly, Series MVP: Randy Johnson and Curt Schilling (co-MVPs)

2002 - Anaheim Angels (now Los Angeles Angels), Manager: Mike Scioscia, Series MVP: Troy Glaus

2003 - Florida Marlins, Manager: Jack McKeon, Series MVP: Josh Beckett

2004 - Boston Red Sox, Manager: Terry Francona, Series MVP: Manny Ramirez

2005 - Chicago White Sox, Manager: Ozzie Guillen, Series MVP: Jermaine Dye

2006 - St. Louis Cardinals, Manager: Tony La Russa, Series MVP: David Eckstein

2007 - Boston Red Sox, Manager: Terry Francona, Series MVP: Mike Lowell

2008 - Philadelphia Phillies, Manager: Charlie Manuel, Series MVP: Cole Hamels

2009 - New York Yankees, Manager: Joe Girardi, Series MVP: Hideki Matsui

2010 - San Francisco Giants, Manager: Bruce Bochy, Series MVP: Edgar Renteria

2011 - St. Louis Cardinals, Manager: Tony La Russa, Series MVP: David Freese

2012 - San Francisco Giants, Manager: Bruce Bochy, Series MVP: Pablo Sandoval

2013 - Boston Red Sox, Manager: John Farrell, Series MVP: David Ortiz

2014 - San Francisco Giants, Manager: Bruce Bochy, Series MVP: Madison Bumgarner

2015 - Kansas City Royals, Manager: Ned Yost, Series MVP: Salvador Perez

2016 - Chicago Cubs, Manager: Joe Maddon, Series MVP: Ben Zobrist

2017 - Houston Astros, Manager: A.J. Hinch, Series MVP: George Springer

2018 - Boston Red Sox, Manager: Alex Cora, Series MVP: Steve Pearce

2019 - Washington Nationals, Manager: Dave Martinez, Series MVP: Stephen Strasburg

2020 - Los Angeles Dodgers, Manager: Dave Roberts, Series MVP: Corey Seager

2021 - Atlanta Braves, Manager: Brian Snitker, Series MVP: Jorge Soler

2022 Houston Astros, Manager: Dusty Baker, Series MVP Jeremy Pena

Note: The World Series MVP award was first given out in 1955, so prior to that year, there is no official Series MVP.

Here is a list of every MLB Award winner since 1900, National League MVPs:

1931: Frank Frisch (St. Louis Cardinals)

1932: Chuck Klein (Philadelphia Phillies)

1933: Carl Hubbell (New York Giants)

1934: Dizzy Dean (St. Louis Cardinals)

1935: Gabby Hartnett (Chicago Cubs)

1936: Carl Hubbell (New York Giants)

1937: Joe Medwick (St. Louis Cardinals)

1938: Ernie Lombardi (Cincinnati Reds)

1939: Bucky Walters (Cincinnati Reds)

1940: Frank McCormick (Cincinnati Reds)

1941: Dolph Camilli (Brooklyn Dodgers)

1942: Mort Cooper (St. Louis Cardinals)

1943: Stan Musial (St. Louis Cardinals)

1944: Marty Marion (St. Louis Cardinals)

1945: Phil Cavarretta (Chicago Cubs)

1946: Stan Musial (St. Louis Cardinals)

1947: Bob Elliott (Boston Braves)

1948: Stan Musial (St. Louis Cardinals)

1949: Jackie Robinson (Brooklyn Dodgers)

1950: Jim Konstanty (Philadelphia Phillies)

1951: Roy Campanella (Brooklyn Dodgers)

1952: Hank Sauer (Chicago Cubs)

1953: Roy Campanella (Brooklyn Dodgers)

1954: Willie Mays (New York Giants)

1955: Roy Campanella (Brooklyn Dodgers)

1956: Don Newcombe (Brooklyn Dodgers)

1957: Hank Aaron (Milwaukee Braves)

1958: Ernie Banks (Chicago Cubs)

1959: Ernie Banks (Chicago Cubs)

1960: Dick Groat (Pittsburgh Pirates)

1961: Frank Robinson (Cincinnati Reds)

1962: Maury Wills (Los Angeles Dodgers)

1963: Sandy Koufax (Los Angeles Dodgers)

1964: Ken Boyer (St. Louis Cardinals)

1965: Willie Mays (San Francisco Giants)

1966: Roberto Clemente (Pittsburgh Pirates

) 1967: Orlando Cepeda (St. Louis Cardinals)

1968: Bob Gibson (St. Louis Cardinals)

1969: Willie McCovey (San Francisco Giants)

1970: Johnny Bench (Cincinnati Reds)

1971: Joe Torre (St. Louis Cardinals)

1972: Johnny Bench (Cincinnati Reds)

1973: Pete Rose (Cincinnati Reds)

1974: Steve Garvey (Los Angeles Dodgers)

1975: Joe Morgan (Cincinnati Reds)

1976: Joe Morgan (Cincinnati Reds)

1977: George Foster (Cincinnati Reds)

1978: Dave Parker (Pittsburgh Pirates)

1979: Keith Hernandez (St. Louis Cardinals)

1980: Mike Schmidt (Philadelphia Phillies)

1981: Mike Schmidt (Philadelphia Phillies)

1982: Dale Murphy (Atlanta Braves)

1983: Dale Murphy (Atlanta Braves)

1984: Ryne Sandberg (Chicago Cubs)

1985: Willie McGee (St. Louis Cardinals)

1986: Mike Schmidt (Philadelphia Phillies)

1987: Andre Dawson (Chicago Cubs)

1988: Kirk Gibson (Los Angeles Dodgers)

1989: Kevin Mitchell (San Francisco Giants)

1990: Barry Bonds (Pittsburgh Pirates)

1991: Terry Pendleton (Atlanta Braves)

1992: Barry Bonds (Pittsburgh Pirates)

1993: Barry Bonds (San Francisco Giants)

1994: Jeff Bagwell (Houston Astros)

1995: Barry Larkin (Cincinnati Reds)

1996: Ken Caminiti (San Diego Padres)

1997: Larry Walker (Colorado Rockies)

1998: Sammy Sosa (Chicago Cubs)

1999: Chipper Jones (Atlanta Braves)

2000: Jeff Kent (San Francisco Giants)

2001: Barry Bonds (San Francisco Giants)

2002: Barry Bonds (San Francisco Giants)

2003: Barry Bonds (San Francisco Giants)

2004: Barry Bonds (San Francisco Giants)

2005: Albert Pujols (St. Louis Cardinals)

2006: Ryan Howard (Philadelphia Phillies)

2007: Jimmy Rollins (Philadelphia Phillies)

2008: Albert Pujols (St. Louis Cardinals)

2009: Albert Pujols (St. Louis Cardinals)

2010: Joey Votto (Cincinnati Reds)

2011: Ryan Braun (Milwaukee Brewers)

2012: Buster Posey (San Francisco Giants)

2013: Andrew McCutchen (Pittsburgh Pirates)

2014: Clayton Kershaw (Los Angeles Dodgers)

2015: Bryce Harper (Washington Nationals)

2016: Kris Bryant (Chicago Cubs)

2017: Giancarlo Stanton (Miami Marlins)

2018: Christian Yelich (Milwaukee Brewers)

2019: Cody Bellinger (Los Angeles Dodgers)

2020: Freddie Freeman (Atlanta Braves)

2021: Bryce Harper (Philadelphia Phillies)

2022: Paul Goldschmidt (St Louis Cardinals)

American League MVPs:

1911: Ty Cobb (Detroit Tigers)

1912: Tris Speaker (Boston Red Sox)

1913: Walter Johnson (Washington Senators)

1914: Eddie Collins (Philadelphia Athletics)

1915: Eddie Collins (Chicago White Sox)

1916: Tris Speaker (Boston Red Sox)

1917: Eddie Collins (Chicago White Sox)

1918: George Sisler (St. Louis Browns)

1919: Walter Johnson (Washington Senators)

1920: George Sisler (St. Louis Browns)

1921: Babe Ruth (New York Yankees)

1922: George Sisler (St. Louis Browns)

1923: Babe Ruth (New York Yankees)

1924: Walter Johnson (Washington Senators)

1925: Roger Peckinpaugh (Washington Senators)

1926: George Burns (Cleveland Indians)

1927: Lou Gehrig (New York Yankees)

1928: Jimmie Foxx (Philadelphia Athletics)

1929: Al Simmons (Philadelphia Athletics)

1930: Joe Cronin (Washington Senators)

1931: Lou Gehrig (New York Yankees)

1932: Jimmie Foxx (Philadelphia Athletics)

1933: Jimmie Foxx (Philadelphia Athletics)

1934: Mickey Cochrane (Detroit Tigers)

1935: Hank Greenberg (Detroit Tigers)

1936: Lou Gehrig (New York Yankees)

1937: Charlie Gehringer (Detroit Tigers)

1938: Jimmie Foxx (Boston Red Sox)

1939: Joe DiMaggio (New York Yankees)

1940: Hank Greenberg (Detroit Tigers)

1941: Joe DiMaggio (New York Yankees)

1942: Joe Gordon (New York Yankees)

1943: Spud Chandler (New York Yankees)

1944: Hal Newhouser (Detroit Tigers)

1945: Hal Newhouser (Detroit Tigers)

1946: Ted Williams (Boston Red Sox)

1947: Joe DiMaggio (New York Yankees)

1948: Lou Boudreau (Cleveland Indians)

1949: Ted Williams (Boston Red Sox)

1950: Phil Rizzuto (New York Yankees)

1951: Yogi Berra (New York Yankees)

1952: Bobby Shantz (Philadelphia Athletics)

1953: Al Rosen (Cleveland Indians)

1954: Yogi Berra (New York Yankees)

1955: Yogi Berra (New York Yankees)

1956: Mickey Mantle (New York Yankees)

1957: Mickey Mantle (New York Yankees)

1958: Jackie Jensen (Boston Red Sox)

1959: Nellie Fox (Chicago White Sox)

1960: Roger Maris (New York Yankees)

1961: Roger Maris (New York Yankees)

1962: Mickey Mantle (New York Yankees)

1963: Elston Howard (New York Yankees)

1964: Brooks Robinson (Baltimore Orioles)

1965: Zoilo Versalles (Minnesota Twins)

1966: Frank Robinson (Baltimore Orioles)

1967: Carl Yastrzemski (Boston Red Sox)

1968: Denny McLain (Detroit Tigers)

1969: Harmon Killebrew (Minnesota Twins)

1970: Boog Powell (Baltimore Orioles)

1971: Vida Blue (Oakland Athletics)

1972: Dick Allen (Chicago White Sox)

1973: Reggie Jackson (Oakland Athletics)

1974: Jeff Burroughs (Texas Rangers)

1975: Fred Lynn (Boston Red Sox)

1976: Thurman Munson (New York Yankees)

1977: Rod Carew (Minnesota Twins)

1978: Jim Rice (Boston Red Sox)

1979: Don Baylor (California Angels)

1980: George Brett (Kansas City Royals)

1981: Rollie Fingers (Milwaukee Brewers)

1982: Robin Yount (Milwaukee Brewers)

1983: Cal Ripken Jr. (Baltimore Orioles)

1984: Willie Hernandez (Detroit Tigers)

1985: Don Mattingly (New York Yankees)

1986: Roger Clemens (Boston Red Sox)

1987: George Bell (Toronto Blue Jays)

1988: Jose Canseco (Oakland Athletics)

1989: Robin Yount (Milwaukee Brewers)

1990: Rickey Henderson (Oakland Athletics)

1991: Cal Ripken Jr. (Baltimore Orioles)

1992: Dennis Eckersley (Oakland Athletics)

1993: Frank Thomas (Chicago White Sox)

1994: No award due to players' strike

1995: Mo Vaughn (Boston Red Sox)

1996: Juan Gonzalez (Texas Rangers)

1997: Ken GriffeyJr. (Seattle Mariners)

1998: Juan Gonzalez (Texas Rangers)

1999: Ivan Rodriguez (Texas Rangers)

2000: Jason Giambi (Oakland Athletics)

2001: Ichiro Suzuki (Seattle Mariners)

2002: Miguel Tejada (Oakland Athletics)

2003: Alex Rodriguez (Texas Rangers)

2004: Vladimir Guerrero (Anaheim Angels)

2005: Alex Rodriguez (New York Yankees)

2006: Justin Morneau (Minnesota Twins)

2007: Alex Rodriguez (New York Yankees)

2008: Dustin Pedroia (Boston Red Sox)

2009: Joe Mauer (Minnesota Twins)

2010: Josh Hamilton (Texas Rangers)

2011: Justin Verlander (Detroit Tigers)

2012: Miguel Cabrera (Detroit Tigers)

2013: Miguel Cabrera (Detroit Tigers)

2014: Mike Trout (Los Angeles Angels)

2015: Josh Donaldson (Toronto Blue Jays)

2016: Mike Trout (Los Angeles Angels)

2017: Jose Altuve (Houston Astros)

2018: Mookie Betts (Boston Red Sox)

2019: Mike Trout (Los Angeles Angels)

2020: Jose Abreu (Chicago White Sox)

2021: Shohei Ohtani (Los Angeles Angels)

2022: Aaron Judge (New York Yankees)

American League:

Here are the Rookie of the Year award winners for both the American League and National League since the award's inception in 1947:

American League:

1947: Jackie Robinson (Brooklyn Dodgers)

1948: Alvin Dark (Boston Braves)

1949: Don Newcombe (Brooklyn Dodgers)

1950: Sam Jethroe (Boston Braves)

1951: Willie Mays (New York Giants)

1952: Joe Black (Brooklyn Dodgers)

1953: Jim Gilliam (Brooklyn Dodgers)

1954: Wally Moon (St. Louis Cardinals)

1955: Bill Virdon (St. Louis Cardinals)

1956: Frank Robinson (Cincinnati Reds)

1957: Tony Kubek (New York Yankees)

1958: Orlando Cepeda (San Francisco Giants)

1959: Willie McCovey (San Francisco Giants)

1960: Ron Hansen (Baltimore Orioles)

1961: Don Schwall (Boston Red Sox)

1962: Tom Tresh (New York Yankees)

1963: Gary Peters (Chicago White Sox)

1964: Tony Oliva (Minnesota Twins)

1965: Curt Blefary (Baltimore Orioles)

1966: Tommie Agee (Chicago White Sox)

1967: Rod Carew (Minnesota Twins)

1968: Stan Bahnsen (New York Yankees)

1969: Lou Piniella (Kansas City Royals)

1970: Thurman Munson (New York Yankees)

1971: Chris Chambliss (Cleveland Indians)

1972: Carlton Fisk (Boston Red Sox)

1973: Al Bumbry (Baltimore Orioles)

1974: Mike Hargrove (Texas Rangers)

1975: Fred Lynn (Boston Red Sox)

1976: Mark Fidrych (Detroit Tigers)

1977: Eddie Murray (Baltimore Orioles)

1978: Lou Whitaker (Detroit Tigers)

1979: John Castino (Minnesota Twins)

1980: Joe Charboneau (Cleveland Indians)

1981: Dave Righetti (New York Yankees)

1982: Cal Ripken Jr. (Baltimore Orioles

) 1983: Ron Kittle (Chicago White Sox)

1984: Alvin Davis (Seattle Mariners)

1985: Ozzie Guillen (Chicago White Sox)

1986: Jose Canseco (Oakland Athletics)

1987: Mark McGwire (Oakland Athletics)

1988: Walt Weiss (Oakland Athletics)

1989: Gregg Olson (Baltimore Orioles)

1990: Sandy Alomar Jr. (Cleveland Indians)

1991: Chuck Knoblauch (Minnesota Twins)

1992: Pat Listach (Milwaukee Brewers)

1993: Tim Salmon (California Angels)

1994: Bob Hamelin (Kansas City Royals)

1995: Marty Cordova (Minnesota Twins)

1996: Derek Jeter (New York Yankees)

1997: Nomar Garciaparra (Boston Red Sox)

1998: Ben Grieve (Oakland Athletics)

1999: Carlos Beltran (Kansas City Royals)

2000: Kazuhiro Sasaki (Seattle Mariners)

2001: Ichiro Suzuki (Seattle Mariners)

2002: Eric Hinske (Toronto Blue Jays)

2003: Angel Berroa (Kansas City Royals)

2004: Bobby Crosby (Oakland Athletics)

2005: Huston Street (Oakland Athletics)

2006: Justin Verlander (Detroit Tigers)

2007: Dustin Pedroia (Boston Red Sox)

2008: Evan Longoria (Tampa Bay Rays)

2009: Andrew Bailey (Oakland Athletics)

2010: Neftali Feliz (Texas Rangers)

2011: Jeremy Hellickson (Tampa Bay Rays)

2012: Mike Trout (Los Angeles

2013: Wil Myers (Tampa Bay Rays)

2014: Jose Abreu (Chicago White Sox)

2015: Carlos Correa (Houston Astros)

2016: Michael Fulmer (Detroit Tigers)

2017: Aaron Judge (New York Yankees)

2018: Shohei Ohtani (Los Angeles Angels)

2019: Yordan Alvarez (Houston Astros)

2020: Kyle Lewis (Seattle Mariners)

2021: Randy Arozarena (Tampa Bay Rays)

2022: Julio Rodriguez (Seattle Mariners)

National League:

1947: Jackie Robinson (Brooklyn Dodgers)

1948: Alvin Dark (Boston Braves)

1949: Don Newcombe (Brooklyn Dodgers)

1950: Sam Jethroe (Boston Braves)

1951: Willie Mays (New York Giants)

1952: Joe Black (Brooklyn Dodgers)

1953: Jim Gilliam (Brooklyn Dodgers)

1954: Wally Moon (St. Louis Cardinals)

1955: Bill Virdon (St. Louis Cardinals)

1956: Frank Robinson (Cincinnati Reds)

1957: Jack Sanford (Philadelphia Phillies)

1958: Orlando Cepeda (San Francisco Giants)

1959: Willie McCovey (San Francisco Giants)

1960: Frank Howard (Los Angeles Dodgers)

1961: Billy Williams (Chicago Cubs)

1962: Ken Hubbs (Chicago Cubs)

1963: Pete Rose (Cincinnati Reds)

1964: Dick Allen (Philadelphia Phillies)

1965: Jim Lefebvre (Los Angeles Dodgers)

1966: Tommy Helms (Cincinnati Reds)

1967: Tom Seaver (New York Mets)

1968: Johnny Bench (Cincinnati Reds)

1969: Ted Sizemore (Los Angeles Dodgers)

1970: Carl Morton (Montreal Expos)

1971: Earl Williams (Atlanta Braves)

1972: Jon Matlack (New York Mets)

1973: Gary Matthews (San Francisco Giants)

1974: Bake McBride (St. Louis Cardinals)

1975: John Montefusco (San Francisco Giants)

1976: Butch Metzger (San Diego Padres)

1977: Andre Dawson (Montreal Expos)

1978: Bob Horner (Atlanta Braves)

1979: Rick Sutcliffe (Los Angeles Dodgers)

1980: Steve Howe (Los Angeles Dodgers)

1981: Fernando Valenzuela (Los Angeles Dodgers)

1982: Steve Sax (Los Angeles Dodgers)

1983: Darryl Strawberry (New York Mets)

1984: Dwight Gooden (New York Mets)

1985: Vince Coleman (St. Louis Cardinals)

1986: Todd Worrell (St. Louis Cardinals)

1987: Benito Santiago (San Diego Padres)

1988: Chris Sabo (Cincinnati Reds)

1989: Jerome Walton (Chicago Cubs)

1990: David Justice (Atlanta Braves)

1991: Jeff Bagwell (Houston Astros)

1992: Eric Karros (Los Angeles Dodgers)

1993: Mike Piazza (Los Angeles Dodgers)

1994: Raul Mondesi (Los Angeles Dodgers)

1995: Hideo Nomo (Los Angeles Dodgers)

1996: Todd Hollandsworth (Los Angeles Dodgers)

1997: Scott Rolen (Philadelphia Phillies)

1998: Kerry Wood (Chicago Cubs)

1999: Scott Williamson (Cincinnati Reds)

2000: Rafael Furcal (Atlanta Braves)

2001: Albert Pujols (St. Louis Cardinals)

2002: Jason Jennings (Colorado Rockies)

2003: Dontrelle Willis (Florida Marlins)

2004: Jason Bay (Pittsburgh Pirates)

2005: Ryan Howard (Philadelphia Phillies)

2006: Hanley Ramirez (Florida Marlins)

2007: Ryan Braun (Milwaukee Brewers

2008: Geovany Soto (Chicago Cubs)

2009: Chris Coghlan (Florida Marlins)

2010: Buster Posey (San Francisco Giants)

2011: Craig Kimbrel (Atlanta Braves)

2012: Bryce Harper (Washington Nationals)

2013: Jose Fernandez (Miami Marlins)

2014 Jacob deGrom (New York Mets)

2015 Kris Bryant (Chicago Cubs)

2016: Corey Seager (Los Angeles Dodgers)

2017: Cody Bellinger (Los Angeles Dodgers)

2018: Ronald Acuna Jr. (Atlanta Braves)

2019: Pete Alonso (New York Mets)

2020: Devin Williams (Milwaukee Brewers)

2021: Jonathan India (Cincinnati Reds)

2022: Michael Harris II (Atlanta Braves)

CHAPTER SIX

THE GAME OF BASEBALL IS IN OUR BLOOD

Over the course of more than a century, people's affections have been won over by the game of baseball. It is a sport that has withstood the test of time and is still developing and expanding with each passing year. Baseball has provided us with some of the most iconic and memorable moments in the annals of sports history, dating all the way back to the game's earliest days.

Throughout the course of this book, we have discussed a number of the most intriguing and unexpected aspects of baseball, ranging from the player with the highest career salary in the history of Major League Baseball to the stadium that is the oldest one that is still in use. We have acquired knowledge regarding the best players who have ever competed in the sport of baseball, as well as their respective records, accomplishments, and the influence they have had on the development of the game.

Statistics are an integral part of baseball, which helps to distinguish it from other sports. The game has a long history of meticulously recording statistics, including batting averages, earned run averages, and stolen base totals. Statistics in baseball are not only an important part of the history of the game, but they are also frequently used to evaluate the performance of individual players. Some of the most well-known statistics, such as Babe Ruth's home run record and Joe DiMaggio's hitting streak, have attained a level of notoriety that stands on its own.

A further fascinating subject that we have investigated is the background of the World Series. Since the first two teams competed in the series in 1903 all the way up until the present day, the World Series has become ingrained in the culture of the United States. We have also gained knowledge regarding the historical significance of the seventh-inning stretch, which is now an integral component of each and every baseball game. The seventh-inning stretch gives fans the opportunity to get some exercise, sing "Take Me Out to the Ballgame," and show their appreciation for the sport they so deeply care about.

The game of baseball has long been an important part of American culture, serving to unite fans who have a common interest in watching and playing the sport. It is a game that has been a source of creativity for a wide variety of people, including musicians, artists, and writers, and it has become a symbol of the American identity. Baseball has also played an important part in the development of the United States, from Jackie Robinson breaking the color barrier to the Boston Red Sox winning the World Series despite the tragedy that occurred during the Boston Marathon.

As we come to the end of this book, it is essential to keep in mind that the world of baseball contains a vast amount of information that has not yet been uncovered. There are always new stories to learn about and new statistics to analyze, and this is true from the minor leagues all the way up to the major leagues. Baseball is a game that can be enjoyed by anyone, from those who are only passingly interested to those who are devoted followers of the sport.

To summarize, baseball is more than just a recreational activity. It is a piece of our cultural heritage, a representation of the identity of the

United States of America, and a source of motivation and happiness for millions of fans all over the world. We hope that by the time you've finished reading this book, you'll have developed a greater appreciation for baseball as a sport as well as its players and will be motivated to continue learning more about the game.

Name: _____

Baseball Teams Crossword Puzzle

Across
2. ST LOUIS
4. ARIZONA
6. CLEVELAND
8. LOS ANGELES
14. MINNESOTA
16. KANSAS CITY
19. PITTSBURGH
20. BOSTON
21. SAN DIEGO
22. HOUSTON
23. TAMPA BAY
24. BALTIMORE
25. TORONTO
26. MILWAUKEE
28. CHICAGO
29. SAN FRANCISCO
30. NEW YORK

Down
1. NEW YORK
3. CINCINNATI
5. TEXAS
7. DETROIT
9. PHILADELPHIA
10. SEATTLE
11. WASHINGTON
12. CHICAGO
13. OAKLAND
15. LOS ANGELES
17. ATLANTA
18. MIAMI
27. COLORADO

Name: _____

Baseball Word Scramble Puzzle 2

1. LWEOHSEEHU ....

2. OUFNG ....

3. MDUON ....

4. DENILEIVR ....

5. WILBLTNI ....

6. RAEHLTE ....

7. ROELRL ....

8. ALICCTS ....

9. MAECOKBCRE ....

10. RASTIFESB ....

11. CLHUTC ....

12. NRAUOIT ....

13. IPOTUFL ....

14. CSJKAKECRRAC ....

15. EMLUBR ....

16. DOERATAG ....

17. TSQA ....

18. EROVGO ....

19. LRHU ....

20. ILRNE ....

Word Bank

mound	lumber	liner	groove
roller	rainout	gatorade	twinbill
wheelhouse	crackerjacks	leather	clutch
hurl	comebacker	firstbase	linedrive
foultip	fungo	cactus	sqat

Name: _____

Baseball Word Search Puzzle 2

```
S  T  I  R  U  P  S  R  W  P  H  C  C  C  V  H  K
O  U  L  J  B  L  T  S  Q  U  E  E  Z  E  A  C  B
F  Y  F  P  C  K  R  B  X  V  Q  L  U  N  A  U  L
F  W  S  Q  A  R  A  E  O  D  N  P  Z  P  A  O  Q
I  X  P  F  I  O  N  W  T  E  Q  U  D  Q  M  W  K
H  U  I  L  Q  D  D  I  L  E  O  I  H  W  B  G  I
W  B  T  S  P  I  K  E  S  K  H  A  Z  F  T  O  V
H  I  B  E  Y  P  F  W  L  E  S  D  W  B  E  U  Y
J  I  A  P  S  H  D  L  Z  D  E  V  N  X  Q  Y  X
J  A  L  C  V  E  T  E  R  A  N  A  F  M  M  O  B
D  I  L  N  W  H  H  T  L  F  Q  N  N  E  F  B  E
R  U  B  B  E  R  C  Q  H  T  A  C  N  A  C  V  A
U  K  A  R  X  H  W  T  O  A  I  E  W  T  F  C  N
R  E  K  C  A  B  E  M  O  C  R  B  O  B  W  G  B
M  A  V  O  I  Y  E  Z  S  P  I  X  R  A  H  S  A
Q  Y  P  U  O  S  K  C  E  D  N  O  D  L  W  V  L
A  C  E  F  B  I  C  O  C  M  D  R  R  L  H  A  L
```

Ace
Advance
Beanball
Comebacker
Deeked
Meatball
Ondeck
Rubber
Spikes
Spitball
Squeeze
Stirups
Strand
Veteran
Whiff

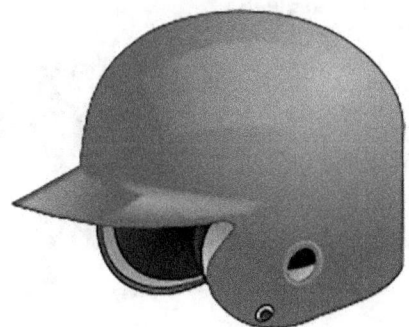

Name: _____

Baseball Crossword Puzzle 3

Across

2. Babe Ruth's real first name

7. Who holds the record for being the oldest MLB baseball player ever

9. What team that plays in New York won the 1986 World Series

10. What team does not play in the U.S

13. What team from the 1970's was nicknamed "The Big Red Machine"

14. The White Sox were originally called the White _____

16. What team plays in Coors Field

17. What team had the worst all time record

Down

1. The first team in major league baseball was the Boston, _____

3. What team plays in Washington and is in the AL West

4. What team holds the single season home run record

5. Clevelands first MLB team was known as the _____

6. What team plays in the NL East and won the 1924 World Series

8. Who is the only Hall of Famer to die in a plane crash

11. What is the Cardinals stadium called

12. Who did win the 2017 World Series

15. Where did the Giants originally play

Name: _____

Baseball Word Search Puzzle 3

```
F G I Q U N K L I W T F F S Z B G   backstop
O Y D Z L U Q S Q W F E T E F A N   Fence
F R E E P A S S R Z D N Q C D T I   Assit
U M F I R S T B A S E C A O P T R   roller
L C M B F L Y B A L L E A N I E T   freepass
L A T E B R O L L E R F J D T R S   foultip
C H N T M L R Z K Q A G E B C S E   shoestring
O B A C K S T O P U E M F A H B O   Battersbox
U G H E E S U C W U C P A S E O H   Sidearm
N F O S V S I D E A R M O E R X S   Fullcount
T V M A A T P U H C P I T L U O F   Home plate
S T E B L D I F O D V G D S A L C   Homerun
Y N P D F V I Z M H Y L V J X T X
P U L R X V K I E A S S I T G I E
```

25 Baseball Puzzles – Template

SPRING TRAINING PARKS

```
J X R O G E R D E A N L X N T G X A T G
F N R E N N E R B N I E T S J S V Q T F
F D R S T J E V X L P Y Y G B U V T I V
S M O C E L Y O V V E L V A E N F T E U
U D N O M M A H M C O X S K X T T S D Y
R T A Q N Y N T F S R X U E N E E A B R
P G C Q S R M D A K I D H J A U V H S A
R K W F W M O R O X A T N M C H U Q D I
I J V S X W W D I P O K U X I L B U P E
S A L T R I V E R F I E L D S S Y W G E
E P L H C N A R K C A B L E M A C K Q K
E D E L E C T R I C P A R K T K Q Q W Y
I S J J K H T I M S D E X K U G P M Y O
E U L B T E J P E J D K T U M F H H A M
K K G A M E R I C A N F A M I L Y J D A
K D S C O T T S D A L E N N Y R D V O K
O L B A I D E P M E T I B T P N F S T O
L K Y B V S J J S L O A N P A R K T L H
I M A U H W G E R A C Y A B Q O Q N O O
K R A P R E V O L C H D O D M S O T O H
G K R A P L L A B D T K Y A C X F H C M
Y G M R P J D H H N D J N A Q N W U A A
J X X M C H A R L O T T E O I W O O V X
S D W T L G O O D Y E A R T A R F R K Q
```

AMERICAN FAMILY	FITTEAM	ROGER DEAN
BAYCARE	GOODYEAR	SALT RIVER FIELDS
CAMELBACK RANCH	HAMMOND	SCOTTSDALE
CHARLOTTE	HOHOKAM	SLOAN PARK
CLOVER PARK	JETBLUE	STEINBRENNER
COOLTODAY	LECOM	SURPRISE
ED SMITH	PEORIA	TD BALLPARK
ELECTRIC PARK	PUBLIX	TEMPE DIABLO

MLB TEAM NAMES

```
P T M M T M S T N A I G Y T W P K Q W Q
I H F A B V D T L D J X A A U L I X M O
C U I H T X E A S C D E N R N S F T R N
T D T L Y H R P U L W P A M E K S I U P
I W Q Q L X L B B S C T M V H E E G S H
K G A H O I S E N M D S A W T C I E H B
O S T S P E E A T S A R W A V H T R S Q
W R D R O L I S T I B I R S E H S S G L
B E I K B D L N N Y C I L N P O E E C M
R G R O N G A B J L P S H F V R X H T U
T D E I L I P T B G S Y A J E U L B V H
O O H U G E F K S S F B Y J G C P U R C
W D W A C S S Q S T L U R S J U F A O P
D T S J V N F S K J D A L T P E N D Y W
M W M N Q I G K C S A A N I R G S H A H
M I G G T L X J A C N K H O E H G D L I
V N D P D R S E B I K B B L I U G Y S T
U S T R F A B A D K T L S O M T M W F E
I T H W T M L R N C T M Y S Y B A Q C S
R Y T N S E A O O G N W E X M R E N L O
Y D N H J C G C M L I U I T U C X K I X
H G S E X M O Y A Q P H R T S M I Y D N
U C M H T G L V I T V T Y U J R H K Y I
N Y A B P Y L E D M A A N H F D Q B W D
```

ANGELS	GIANTS	PIRATES
ATHLETICS	GIANTS	RED SOX
BLUE JAYS	INDIANS	REDS
BRAVES	MARLINS	ROYALS
CARDINALS	METS	TIGERS
CUBS	NATIONALS	TWINS
DIAMONDBACKS	ORIOLES	WHITE SOX
DODGERS	PHILLIES	YANKEES

SCORING TERMS

```
D S E L G N I S D L E I F N I Y K F H I
H F A X D G U S D Y V S A Q G L A B P D
F C J A S C B U P K F Q P X R F G R C R
P A T E A T R D V J V Y W P O E W A C O
O N M I A L C E V W I H D O U C N I N P
Y P X A P B T R I I V W U H N I F C F P
F U U O H Y U R V U S L C N D F G V E E
F Y F E D K B C U F B S V U R I G M L D
I C H T L C F T P B U N T R U R A A P B
E G R C C U B L I U X R E E L C P W I A
L F O A T V R C E H Q H F M E A J U R L
D L R T T I C Y W M G I E O D S Q D T L
E K R Q R I P J L R O N V H O X X N E A
R J E W J J H D A F I H D O U B L E L C
S P Y K A J H N L L D A L W B U R N U T
C Y Y X J L D B E I W L O A L X I F R W
H W E E I S K H E C W I E F E E N I D E
O E E L L G T U G L P V X I Y T E M N A
I R A A P N I G X K G D B O F U S C U X
C K M L W I P V J R L N R S O N Y O O H
E S B O A D R U H D Q A I L G Y I X R B
H V D S I F P T X B P V B S P Y L O G I
L I N S I D E T H E P A R K F R N U N W
W A L K O F F V R B Y H O M B D W J R L
```

BALK	GRAND SLAM	INSIDE THE PARK
BUNT	GROUND RULE DOUBLE	SACRIFICE FLY
DOUBLE	GROUND RULE TRIPLE	SINGLE
DOWN THE LINE	HIT	STEAL HOME
DROPPED BALL	HIT BY PITCH	TRIPLE
ERROR	HOME RUN	WALK
FIELDERS CHOICE	INFIELD FLY RULE	WALK-OFF
GAP	INFIELD SINGLE	WILD PITCH

RECENT AMERICAN LEAGUE ALL-STARS

```
T W E N D L E Y N O G G A I C R A G R K
A V D A J M W W X U Y Y E G G J M I O U
C K S O N A G A O R C O R R E A J G H X
S U I G E F A L L B O G A E R T S L L Y
J P J A I I L I Q S D E D G O T M W I S
Q D D L M B L S T J H K O A E Y R H E G
P L B U E R O R U O V B K C Y P E J F R
K E Y H S A I E O W L O M D E E T O P L
A I Y D B N B U R N A E D R X H T W W F
L F K L Q T N D T C N L E X S X E K S A
T I K R D L O L G O E Z N W B C H Y D D
U R I K D E G Q M Y R G H P L E C S H G
V R E Z E Y G U E R R E R O O Q I S Y E
E E C I U B U O Y F N S Q G R A B T N H
L M B Y Q N I U W U O H P E H O S S L I
W E B L U X I Y V S S L A Y B A R D N U
I O D F G I B N E I R F S D B E C L G I
P B R Y R R L G O P E D Q O V A V P X K
E J N V T M D E J S D W D E N Z K R J D
N G W R Y U V Y I S N N D K U H H M P O
R U J W J D K M T I A C P R S K I J S N
P W Z E D N A N R E H B C S Y Y Y M X D
X H W P Z E R I M A R X L S N I L L U M
F K N P U M E M A R T I N E Z J S J V L
```

ALTUVE	GALLO	OLSON
ANDERSON	GARCIA	PEREZ
BICHETTER	GUERRERO	RAMIREZ
BOGAERTS	HERNANDEZ	SEMIEN
BRANTLEY	JUDGE	TROUT
CORREA	MARTINEZ	WALSH
CRUZ	MERRIFIELD	WENDLE
DEVERS	MULLINS	ZUNINO

RECENT NATIONAL LEAGUE ALL-STARS

```
V V R E B R A W H C S G B V J O G F F X
S W C A S T E L L A N O S D O Q H I I K
W Q R E I Z A R F V S U A D K C S H Q H
M F R E E M A N C C T T A Y D A D V V S
M V F I D S W W D F W N T D S Y L X O F
U N I K W E H F V W E A Q S G E O C T C
N U N B M L G P F R W Y L F E A N Q U O
C S Q V Y W J K A X C J N Y V K Y R M B
Y K T X S H L S R M E M I P L H E N L M
U V W A M B P B W H F S Y J O E R G A F
K B B T N H A L E I X F C V K S W X E T
R A E K G P N N Y T N D W O C X E C R A
I L J W A B I I F X T K R O B D D Y A Y
D B M P C K L A E E D S E O F A E B E L
M I Y Y U G O B C E Q F T R F L R C D O
R E N I N D M J V G F F X S W W C Q A R
E S O B A H H T R O W E N O R C A J V P
N O R R B R D U A N A R V A E Z C R H F
R N U Y F O T O S Y K V L H H E I K C U
U P L A J C O D A H C A M T D V R U K Q
T P W N Y A U H V R Q H B K G B O M D J
D V P T T S H W G F H M N L P R P H R W
G S I T A T X D S S D W I M J F Y V Y B
L Y O S S R B M P S H U M U V W S F S O
```

ACUNA	ESCOBAR	REALMUTO
ALBIES	FRAZIER	REYNOLDS
ARENADO	FREEMAN	SCHWARBER
BETTS	MACHADO	SOTO
BRYANT	MOLINA	TATIS
CASTELLANOS	MUNCY	TAYLOR
CRAWFORD	NARVAEZ	TURNER
CRONEWORTH	POSEY	WINKER

MOST VALUABLE TRADING CARDS

```
P N L R S L M Q V R L Q H W V F R R W N
S M A I L L I W J A O O S R D G K E J R
Y C C N Y W R S J I L B U X S I F L F L
G Y C F T H Y O H I J F I Y Y U N T E E
B C X E J H I G A A M X K N R O E N P Y
R F K N D E U M E Q M S Q D S L Y A D K
M U S I A L H A Q L S A J S C O G M H E
B I A J I E O W J Q F A T H D P N W S Q
H E T N E M E L C I S N P H A V H Y X Y
R L W C Q G V O Q K E C K F E A O M E P
B S K I O D H D U U Y D N R O W R D L B
K N W X Y O S G L R O U A T P M S O B O
N U W E E X T F U Y T P L O L J F O N W
K M S X H I P V L O V O P J T O S N N O
W M E L N T G E T T G S V F D H U F R K
T R G E M T A A E E J N U R M N N K T F
W H I C R O O M M U E O E R V S R X W A
E M A N J C J M L C D G H B J O Q U T P
S L P L Y D I M A G G I O Y H N S D J E
N C C O E Q K P F U S E D H T K Y I U V
J N U B U Y L I G E H R I G U D A E N W
G N K E B T X F E G X B F A R G M G N P
G Q S L S O P H E X P K M R E N G A W L
X O U H H U C F L J A C K S O N S P X Q
```

AARON	JOHNSON	PAFKO
BENGOUGH	LAJOIE	PAIGE
CLEMENTE	MAGIE	PLANK
COBB	MANTLE	ROBINSON
DIMAGGIO	MATHEWS	RUTH
DOYLE	MATHEWSON	WAGNER
GEHRIG	MAYS	WILLIAMS
JACKSON	MUSIAL	YOUNG

TAKE ME OUT TO THE BALL GAME

```
C D F S Q O U V U E P A G T K A Y I U U
B Q G L W U A D B N E V J T B M X C W F
U Y E N R S P T A G B R B K C A B E N J
W U V K M T P I W S R P H P H I K R V T
A B T T N Y L S P F X G S T M R P F V U
C R O W D M Y B G S B H R A E W T O V M
V M P R N R Y X A Y C M B O O N E N C D
F H A O K J A B R M O C N E L E K E X J
V D T P E I K E S T U N A E P C Q V S A
P N Y Q C M L J P E L D D O A H W E S A
W G J T U R A V O U D C F J J E K K Q Y
H P K W L O S H M K T E U P R I F D B H
I I I C E G M T S G U Q G Y R H T U S T
W F M M K C N Y R I O G S T B I Y A L N
P T O A P W T W F E Q E S A E L Q S L E
O H Y U E H A C O W T X T M B E C S T V
E G H O T T R A G Q Q C Q E O T O J A E
I H O Q V W C R A Y H E H G M Q O D P S
B E W I N V K E M N U V G R N V K O L R
B K T B E G U T E A G E F H G I J T R O
L I V U J L A M O I P R L J H B N S T O
L V H Y B K N M A L X L J R K S M N Y E
A I Q O E H F R N R E F T Y E H T E I E
B I B X M T Q B Q N P L P P O X P M V E
```

BACK	INNING	SHAME
BALL	JACK	STRETCH
BUY	OLD	STRIKES
CARE	ONE	TAKE
CROWD	OUT	TEAM
EVER	PEANUTS	THEY
GAME	ROOT	THREE
HOME	SEVENTH	TWO

NATIONAL LEAGUE CITIES

```
S P X A T D Y N O T G N I H S A W D P U
A B M O Q W S S J H G R U B S T T I P H
N M N G G B E E L X F C R K S M R G L S
D I P F D S R L U T F D M Y O A C G C T
I L N R T Q D E H C K H Q H T K L A I L
E W M E T S A G B A D N D E P V R K M O
G A M T W L P N A C B Y S F V D M Q S U
O U G R J P P A K E O H P G I C I U E I
W K Q V A P N S G W J S W N D R A Y J S
Q E U U K G N O K U E O A P M Q M Q V F
N E E H K G T L A H P L F T T B I E D A
E B R M O C H F L L S L S E I L L I H P
W G Q W R H C H I C A G O W W F R S X B
Y K A I H P L E D A L I H P V O G R B Y
O S R E W E R B L B H Y Y B R A V E S N
R K V A V D A J A S E X U E K S D E R A
K Q A R U F B O T N S J R L O O D F E T
C D M S O V E O L M N S S S M X D X O I
E D M Y B A F B A R I V H G R U Y L T O
H R Y K V U A V N D L S R E G D O D A N
J A E F B F C M T S R U T W H D P U J A
K S V O D Y X U A V A M V X W P H T S L
E Y Q J W B Q I R L M F K N D C T R E S
G L X G Y J Q V I T A N N I C N I C N K
```

ATLANTA	LOS ANGELES	PHILADELPHIA
BRAVES	MARLINS	PHILLIES
BREWERS	METS	PIRATES
CARDINALS	MIAMI	PITTSBURGH
CHICAGO	MILWAUKEE	REDS
CINCINNATI	NATIONALS	SAN DIEGO
CUBS	NEW YORK	ST LOUIS
DODGERS	PADRES	WASHINGTON

AMERICAN LEAGUE CITIES

```
F H T I G E R S A O X T R Q S U M E G I
Q U Y F A F T F K K O O X O E E A M Y A
S F V M Q C M R E H S R L S G T R E L R
E D H D P A O K F D D O J K H G I M S A
A Y C S T Y O N H J E N Q T M B N W V N
T U L M W V H T A Y R T K D K E E U H C
T E O E M U A J I I M O R C F R R Q C S
L F N D P M X L Q X C U H O R G S N K N
E U K J P K H L L J S R O P I A O C B A
W R A A J U J F Y C D O U J L T Y K U I
B K B B B Q B N C R H O S A I C V V S D
A A P S L A Y O R N A F T W C L Q V Y R
Y N B O S T O N L K R S O R T S A O A A
J S J U I F B I L Y F O N X C D A R J U
E A O E J S M A P S A O C B I Q Y I E G
U S N G C S N F D B C N D S V S G O U L
J C J J A D C J D N T N K J A P O L L W
D I D J M C V I A R A Y S E S F Q E B A
X T D S A Q I R T L D J S I E P M S W Y
J Y E A E L M H E E U N Q B V S C C Q Y
A C Q E M L I V C E L O Q R F L J P P I
D N T O F O E O W J K H P M U A R Q V F
D V X L V L D O A W H I T E S O X E Y H
R B R U C W E R O M I T L A B S W E D F
```

ASTROS	GUARDIANS	RED SOX
ATHLETICS	HOUSTON	ROYALS
BALTIMORE	KANSAS CITY	SEATTLE
BLUE JAYS	MARINERS	TAMPA BAY
BOSTON	NEW YORK	TIGERS
CHICAGO	OAKLAND	TORONTO
CLEVELAND	ORIOLES	WHITE SOX
DETROIT	RAYS	YANKEES

MLB GOLD GLOVE AWARD WINNERS

```
H Q G V O R L X D H W K U N P O O N K Y
P O W E R L U S S I A O G A L X U Q R O
S C A M P A N E L L A C R S D N O B N K
H H I R J M P G I R T S B E M B Y T I F
E U V H C E L N O P I O O I C H E N I T
R H B K P Q E D V T M A Z E R O S K I S
D M B S F R R T R E N O F G M X T U P I
X A P Y B I L B T W B B I O W U R X R R
O Y K X G Q L N D O E Q F T P O Z G O B
H S K U M O V B I S N Y Y T N R E X B O
M D E S L T G C M H C W M R X P M B I Z
E Z I P X L V D H I H T E X S U S L N U
E I E A X E F H C G C M I T V P K E S F
N J C Q H G W W S O L N M Y N W I X O R
H E R N A N D E Z Q E P C K I E Q J N R
G R A F B R P C A P A R I C I O M G R B
L E E H R G X F O Z E H C N A S H E Y T
B G X T B R U R N L R Q A Y C H V I L U
P N W I F H A J F E S B V S H F M Y C C
I A N M N I S F O E E B Y O I B H D S R
Q L I S M D I G V D N G O R D O N T U M
X E V X X U F O Y A O D B B X U D D A M
N B W W H I T E V Y J C G R E I N K E Q
K Q Y M P K E R U T R R J E G M Y P V W
```

APARICIO	HERNANDEZ	ROBINSON
BELANGER	JONES	RODRIGUEZ
BENCH	KALINE	SANCHEZ
BONDS	KNOOP	SCHMIDT
CAMPANELLA	MADDUX	SMITH
CLEMENTE	MAYS	WHITE
GORDON	MAZEROSKI	YESTRZEMSKI
GREINKE	POWER	ZOBRIST

GREATEST HITTERS

```
S E I E Q N W M G L G V U B A E W S X T
L G A I J M F T O V U H S O X N F C P N
G M G L A I S U M L E A U X E Y T D N M
O V W U M C A C G N I E J K M L E R Y I
L S Y K H X O F D O X T P J G S H X V C
M A Y S D B X E W U F I O T O H B P K N
P I P M B F R D W I R K G R H S K Q R E
X R W D Q S J R K E N H T T X G Y K E I
P R I P O C F M W R Y A A R O N V O N O
G C K N C T E M L T M C B I A J D I G Y
J S S G F O Q R T L R H V K E C D G A M
H E M K W I I I I E O W B N V F C G W P
X L E A F B R K C B D M A T D B N I V R
C O Z C O T G D R A R Q N N Y W G B U B
D N R R O K A E Y E I G S F D A V T D J
K S T V E L Q D R O Q G O E F Q H F G J
O M S K L K L M F Y U K N K F O Y B E Y
H N A G N S A I R S E X L D I M R T K P
F G Y X G R D E N J Z N B J G O E K T X
R J G N N O W I P S L P L R C R R B C D
A T B Y W N B O S S U P D K D B B V V I
T U O Y P U J O L S N I Q D W C Y J O S
R X T X P A L M E I R O K N C F M S E C
W Y P R I M T V H T G U T S U Z U K I I
```

AARON	GWYNN	RIPKEN
ANSON	HENDERSON	RODRIQUEZ
BELTRE	JETER	ROSE
BIGGIO	MAYS	RUTH
BOGGS	MOLITOR	SPEAKER
BROCK	MUSIAL	SUZUKI
COBB	PALMEIRO	WAGNER
COLLINS	PUJOLS	YASTRZEMSKI

GREATEST PITCHERS

```
E E B L W S A B A T H I A I U A E C U F
A L E U Z N E L A V F Q Y A D A L L A H
R Q C T I N K A X C G C R Q J J M Y W S
J P K M I W Y N G N I L L I H C S C J G
X Q F V R Y A N P Q M G L J J P J X C C
Q G A Q J M Y S S N P X A F U O K T Y J
V L B F D P E L D D O O A W S H E S W C
G M H K O V U D Z Q M S X R S A S C A B
E A C O W S M E K D E U N O Q F M G H U
F D J K J G N E R O D U P H E G U U S M
D J E J G I R Y V D G R P L O C F J R G
V R Y G T Q S O A S R W L D H J U X E A
G Q E R B D X M V E T E Q N P O Q K K R
G Q A D A M U T Z E R B X F B O V M L N
C M X L N O J R L S Y P N O T L R A C E
Q D E D S A E W J R I X Q T N H M P F R
E V T G I H L N F N B L S X P N I P S M
D Y J Q C T D R J I R X A B L A G T T I
J R T S M G C B E Y A W R R T H T K R Q
Z T L O M S W W Q V C O E J A V H Q E K
E J M C S E A V E R A N V F J O L M B B
B N H S F C X F H R V G I H J G N U O Y
N N S W B E H D Q W E M R B W Q E M R L
I E O J G M R K S N E M E L C J K E R K
```

BUMGARNER	JOHNSON	SABATHIA
CARLTON	KERSHAW	SCHERZER
CLEMENS	KOUFAX	SCHILLING
DRYSDALE	MADDUX	SEAVER
FELLER	MARTINEZ	SMOLTZ
GLAVINE	RIVERA	VALENZUELA
GROVE	ROBERTS	VERLANDER
HALLADAY	RYAN	YOUNG

ABC'S

```
Q J F M G A X A S F K P T F L O P A O U
Y Q H C S W T X B A S E S L O A D E D M
W U V P R E V Y I Q I L O I Y M O K E P
J N D Y M L D L L A B N A E B E R K A X
X M V Y T V V R P A K D H B B W V V X G
F F L C E N T E R F I E L D E R P H X X
C U R V E B A L L C G G P Y O B T A B O
D S L M L I V R P N G A M A J D G V I R
B S R E A K G V I V C T O N C P D I J P
E I E L W A H N T T L B U N Y K R I F M
S I T P U V N C N G Q A H H R H Y C G E
A Y T J I U I A C Y Q T C E B O R U A C
B C A E R A C R Y F M T H E U Q H D T M
V S B E Y X K D J F A C L X L F C L H R
S E S S A D P E W C T L T E L V H B L N
S A P A S S I S T A A P O T P X A X E T
B D X D P B P R C B C F J A E M M C T N
S Q E E H T R N E F F H I B N L P U E U
H R E T T I H H C T U L C P L F I Q K B
B K D L E I F R E T N E C H N M O E X S
M B F F O X H A W E X X K U R Q N C O O
R J P S T L L A B E S A B L E A Y D C Q
L D G K J W N K B U L C F G A I U M P G
L Y I K G B I Q N G R L Q L B B J H A U
```

ASSIST	BASES LOADED	CATCH
AT BAT	BAT	CATCHER
ATHLETE	BATBOY	CENTER FIELD
BALK	BATTER	CENTER FIELDER
BALL	BEANBALL	CHAMPION
BASE	BULLPEN	CLUB
BASEBALL	BUNT	CLUTCH HITTER
BASERUNNING	CARD	CURVEBALL

STADIUM FOODS

```
X K D R V Q G I H Y S H U T H D G N P B
J P S A I G X I T F R X R A S O M M P R
U W P V G O D T O H L A M U C S C W A H
K V N H I C R Q L D I B N A R T O K D T
O Q R S C A A P S L U F I E U W T N O R
N A R G E N R A M R L V G W D C T I S U
A H V Q C D X I G O C N D L R P O P F G
C L O V R Y X E W J I J A A E E N U H O
H N S P E I R E I F Q L C X L A C P W Y
O O C X A P R N N P N K K U R N A F G N
D U L J M S T E A A E V X T J U N Q X E
O I T N E R K H G R D P E D U T D O J Z
X K J E K C S C J R M Y I B C S Y W Q O
M J D J I O A A A E U U U C F A K X E R
E S B H K M C C A E D B Q A K Y T S W F
D Y C W N K O H J M G W E K M L I B N U
C N C F S B R X Q J D W K S Y X E W R F
O Q Y M P Q K D U D V C O T E E K S O J
R J M U G E L B B U B K T R R E S X C X
N U E G P T X U H C I W D N A S H Q P B
D X A S O I Y C M T M O E H C J S C O C
O T M G K W A T E R H C W D O O D Q P E
G P R E T Z E L S J K B A R B E C U E Q
J M X U S K C I T S A L L E R A Z Z O M
```

BARBECUE	CRACKER JACKS	PICKLES
BEER	FROZEN YOGURT	POPCORN
BUBBLEGUM	HAMBURGER	PRETZELS
CANDY	HOT DOG	SANDWICH
CHEESEBURGER	ICE CREAM	SODA
CHICKEN FINGERS	MOZZARELLA STICKS	SUNFLOWER SEEDS
CORN DOG	NACHO	TRAIL MIX
COTTON CANDY	PEANUTS	WATER

TEAM NAMES

```
B I J N S B X G W S E R D A P V S D L F
R E C N Y O A T S D E R M J W U C S L L
S U J S C F P Y X S V R E K U R N E M S
Y U B Y X N X R M X G J E A M G H I E H
A Q O P A H X G G V S D E X S R S K M C
R A S C A R D I N A L S J E R Y T C Y D
N W F W C Y O C G T S A V R A O R O D Q
A C R E N G X I E I U A K J M R Y R M V
T B M S E T A R I P R K E Q P I H X R S
I P I I M W T D U B L U O I N O E H A R
O H S E J W R I G O L D D G F L M N F E
N T T I Q K V A G B L A B E O E D Y R G
A S C Q V L M M J L F T R N S S Q P Q I
L L C U B S L O T Y E H I V N F V P N T
S A N G A L S N S C G L A E D F R F Q C
U Y D X M W R D R S W E P S R E G D O D
L O H U S A A B E I E T M T W I N S S D
K R Q X N S I A N S I I B H S J U V V V
R T W G F L T C I N C C I U N I V A Y A
O J E B F E T K R I P S G D D P P M V M
L R I R A G L S A L B M S R E W E R B K
S Q G Y A N C P M R J A U W F Y R W G W
S D M L Y A J W M A R S N A I D N I S S
L U Q N C W R F Q M K F S W V W S Y S T
```

ANGELS	DODGERS	PIRATES
ATHLETICS	INDIANS	RANGERS
BLUE JAYS	MARINERS	RAYS
BRAVES	MARLINS	REDS
BREWERS	METS	ROCKIES
CARDINALS	NATIONALS	ROYALS
CUBS	ORIOLES	TIGERS
DIAMONDBACKS	PADRES	TWINS

4 LETTER BASEBALL WORDS

```
L N P U G E D T K W Y M J X V N F G B E
B P P N H O L N M L P I P B R N G W I B
S A D O S G D S T T U F Q D D R A C Q W
K C U N B E T C O X U O Q Q D F M H I R
I C E R S V C R I A F B F S J D A B B T
N S X A F D L L N G O W Q K X T I Q Q R
T M B Q Y S K L P E X L V P B F I R G J
C F B N D J C C F H N S X U L R N W C W
M R C D G L I E X P L I L I A A L B Y H
Q T K N P L A V U R A C N E L B Y C R J
I M L F U A F F B P J H G O X A E Q J T
H T A A C H R Q T K X J Y L M L M M F O
R P W B Y X O K F Y O F N Q L L A H T S
W E L O F C D M W Q D Y X P V O G I C Y
U M G E J C X J D O E S N E U S U U A N
X O K C E D C S O V G N Q T H T U N L U
J H Q Q I L O S A F D W S J T E G L L C
U I G Y I K F S I F S T R I L E H L I F
B H W N S P J C W G R K M G O L I K Y A
I G U L V W H N W N Q B O L S J T N J P
X E A E X X K M N I E Q W R E C S E R P
D M B T F D B B B N H N M Y B U H W C S
J R D Y K B U N T I N F I C X A S W D B
K P T B P S I L V K E G J L F K A G G A
```

BALL   FOUL   MITT
BASE   GAME   NINE
BUNT   GEAR   OUTS
CALL   HALL   PARK
CARD   HITS   PLAY
CLUB   HOME   SAVE
DECK   LINE   SLAM
FAIR   LOSE   WALK

FUNNY NICKNAMES

```
L V O L W V K S K C U D R E B B U R S L
S E I N O P E L B M U R C V O X T D Y W
F T D T W N C X V L J C R W O G A D O M
M Y B J E M S N D I U S A S K E M B B U
T R H I L L C A T S R E A R H K F J W V
D E G R U S D N I W A U W R J I L E O K
W N J H O O K S U S Q E E A W T X W C S
T K E V B F N B L A B M E O H D G E E K
T I N C A P S D S F M O L N N O T C C K
F S G I P N O R I A N T O G E J O T A B
S R A Y X O S J H K H K A R X G P S P A
T A T R G C D O B X O W Q A D X S H S M
I I S A W P A X U A S J D S B I Q R J U
U L E W U H D U B N I A R S Y T E A M D
C R L H B H W I A C D E H H J X S U I C
S A D I D S A Q H P L S S O U P D U A A
I I O D S A R M M L K E G P A M I H E T
B D O E H P C J I C X S A P L O O N S S
K E P H R Q G R G E R J I E L B O Y O L
C R D Q T K D X Q G S T T R L B Y D P N
M S O C P B D X U J A S J S L F J F C A
B Q S S P S R E K C E P D O O W S R T N
B M D P M I R H S O B M U J S K C N F C
T R A S H P A N D A S E H S W K I W F F
```

AQUASOX	HOOKS	RUMBLE PONIES
BISCUITS	IRONPIGS	SODPOODLES
BLUEWAHOOS	JUMBO SHRIMP	SOUNDS
CRAWDADS	LOONS	SPACECOWBOYS
DRILLERS	MUDCATS	TINCAPS
GRASSHOPPERS	RAILRAIDERS	TRASHPANDAS
HAMMERHEADS	RAWHIDE	WINDSURGE
HILLCATS	RUBBERDUCKS	WOODPECKERS

STADIUM SPONSORS

```
C H A S E U R B E V A U S H P P G U E U
E O O C T E P S E L O I R O D G E K L X
N T T D I A M E T U N I M A D G R V A I
O J Y E O V A I E X P A V A C P M U E O
P C X W C K B R H G E P I X J I Q J G A
B N A C I R E M A T A E R G X G T V V C
O Y M Y A T A N D T T A R G E T F I M I
J M R A L U L L E C S U D Q F J Y K B R
Y T N A M F F U A K V F C E I X V U L E
C V X R V D B A S R E H V P L V I R Q M
N S H O L U T P P N C F N H E A V E Q O
T L F U T C E Q W S T W K C B I L N B C
R A O F V E R A U J W A R K O W R R H N
O N O S G V Y B Q A E Q O N L D U U M R
P O I N J I T U K L J H H H G W B T S C
I I Y E S S A W Y Y B T Q Y S R L H R U
C T J Z Y S F N P B F T Q F N I W F E S
A A D I S E V N B E C P O I R G D M G K
N N M T M R E J N L R B C S L L N B O M
A A Y I Q G H J E S H E E B A E E Q R X
V E E C G O Y M F R O S F D C Y N F C G
F S N I L R A M B O C S A N F S T F P C
P V D U T P V F B O N D S J J I L O A F
I R W R I N X F I C K M G X D V D P Q U
```

AT AND T	GLOBE LIFE	PROGRESSIVE
BUSCH	GREAT AMERICAN	ROGERS
CHASE	KAUFFMAN	SAFECO
CITI	MARLINS	TARGET
CITIZENS	MINUTE MAID	TROPICANA
COMERICA	NATIONALS	TURNER
COORS	ORIOLES	US CELLULAR
FENWAY	PETCO	WRIGLEY

MASCOTS

```
N I C U R I K J H K E V B K N J U M D N
W T T M R M E T U F G V O A E E D N X A
S L U G G E R R R V Q X M N M F J A O S
Y X H C E E R C S O Q L B S T H T A L C
B X J L U A V V L D E T U E R N N M A I
X Q U D M G H F Y R W F M G E F P R E T
D N O M Y A R I R I X B S A W P V O S A
P A B Q K T Y A R B I L U S E K R S U N
L N J B T V B R V D V N O U R M E I O A
D Y L G O O E P Q E W N E A B X P E L H
J T I R K G H P P R J E B S E M P R L P
I T Y B N T X T O F N S B E I M A E E E
R I N I P O C Y F P R G R H N C G D F I
H K D Q A L Q T I B R O T T R C A I K L
A J K X J W E S T R U Y U Y E P C C P L
D D A R O B Q M Y V R D H C B R E W B I
A T A C B O B E H T R E T X A B V D U H
W L B C R O D A H C U L S K C A B D N P
X P Q B I L L Y T H E M A R L I N G J T
O A R P C E S O O M R E N I R A M X K G
M W R U B H P D B N W W M R J Q D B H X
S S C V J V T O R R A P E T A R I P W J
S K R E D I L S E Q U Q Q L W V I K F T
R A I R F G N I G N I W S J H S Y U W R
```

ACE	FREDBIRD	PIRATE PARROT
BARRELMAN	GAPPER	RAYMOND
BAXTER THE BOBCAT	LOU SEAL	ROSIE RED
BERNIE BREWER	MARINER MOOSE	SCREECH
BILLY THE MARLIN	MR MET	SLIDER
DBACKS LUCHADOR	ORBIT	SLUGGERRR
DINGER	PAWS	SWINGING FRIAR
DJ KITTY	PHILLIE PHANATIC	THE SAUSAGES

POSITIONS

```
U B H C A O C E S A B T S R I F N P J O
V J K C K F D L E I F T H G I R L V E B
D Y B E L L L H C A O C G N I H C T I P
E N R S R E F D R I H T C N Q V U O G A
S A U R J F P I T C H E R C H V E S T R
I T I X B T S H I T T I N G C O A C H Y
G P M K E F T M D G O A S S E C O N D T
N E A A N I A A F O L U U H R D B B P C
A R N Q C E R G L D K D I A A F A D L G
T E A O H L T L C P C Q N F I S N M G E
E H G S C D I C R K F J U T E Y A J C N
D C E L O J N D E U R J J R C U F C N E
H T R U A S G S Y N M E U F A V D I R R
I I R R C D P O A D T N H M S T S T O A
T P S E H T I F N J N E I C K L N U N L
T F T T C S T C R E D F R U T T X H U M
E E S T K R C L R A W O S F N A D C B A
R I M A S I H O O Q S P G S I V C A T N
E L Y B L F E S W O C K F V W E N O G A
U E U T E P R E X M Q O M M C H L C X G
L R Y W B O T R Y A K B H E F U O D H E
M H C A O C E S A B D R I H T H H U H R
G G B F J J F V S H O R T S T O P X Q A
X R H C A O C N E P L L U B K P X X I B
```

BASERUNNER	DESIGNATED HITTER	PITCHING COACH
BATTER	FIRST	RELIEF PITCHER
BENCH COACH	FIRST BASE COACH	RIGHT FIELD
BULLPEN COACH	GENERAL MANAGER	SECOND
CATCHER	HITTING COACH	SHORTSTOP
CENTER FIELD	LEFT FIELD	STARTING PITCHER
CLOSER	MANAGER	THIRD
COACH	PITCHER	THIRD BASE COACH

PITCHERS

```
S D S R E T T I L P S R U U W K J G W G
A H K I F R U S K D A F S Q Y W P S N A
P V U K W H A X F C E E P H U S Y Y R C
L L A B W E R C S U T B T Y W X F Y J L
T U O D N U O R G R O P P V S B J N O X
B L L Y Q Q S R J V D Y E V A E V S A W
X U K R E D I L S E T W R L K E S P N C
L L A B K R O F D B L E L W M H U A J R
I M A C Q G G V I A B M F H R C C K N H
N U W T C T I K E L I R K E H V U Y J I
S N E I G J O V U L E C K K W T J R A T
H U V S T R I K E N H N S L D Y H O B B
U K R T P K X D P F I M X A Q U X O D Y
T N U B Y E V I U S W U Y B A A I F Q P
O U C F O U R S E A M F A S T B A L L I
U C E D L X O E G C C R V C H U N M X T
T K L A S V P O N N U C E F G J H V J C
T L K J A C V R A K T U M I I J C C W H
M E C Y V F A O H L T Y L F A J E V V W
Y B U X E K R V C A E A N S D G S F M I
S A N J B D S X W W R A P B X A C G K N
J L K O W G A I L C W L V K E X T P N K
Q L L E L L A B T S A F M A E S O W T W
S W I L D P I T C H N T B C J V G Y C E
```

BALK	GROUNDOUT	SINKER
BALL	HIT BY PITCH	SLIDER
CHANGEUP	KNUCKLE-CURVE	SPLITTER
CURVEBALL	KNUCKLEBALL	STRIKE
CUTTER	LOSS	TWO-SEAM FASTBALL
EEPHUS	SAVE	WALK
FORKBALL	SCREWBALL	WILD PITCH
FOUR-SEAM FASTBALL	SHUTOUT	WIN

EQUIPMENT

```
F Q S D X G T J K N E E S A V E R S Y V
T H I R D B A S E M Q S W C V U S P H E
S M L J X A G I L M P H A U C A U N H S
S K H N N S H D I C V M S B R H T E W A
A I E C B E G G R B Q D L P T G N C Y B
B L G T B B A H L A D G J V M S L E B D
D F T A N A T M Y L O O U P A E R D X N
P K T S P L E P D L V B P T A S O I V O
N U I P Q L M S A K E U E T B A O C F C
O L M E Y C L I E N L Q S R M K C O N E
I R S L E A E T Q V T E O V O A J M O S
T W R H S P H D B S O S G V E C J V T O
C F E O R G S H G D Y L W G A Q S A T C
E X H M E C R Y L U M G G W U S G C Q T
T A T E J Q E R H C P U E G T A M D N C
O F A P S H H I G P I W P O N A R N M R
R U C L F K C K K Y Q F H A F I B D O M
P K S A B A T T E R S B O X R U T O S Q
T K K T O W A A A I E E R I P M U T I G
S R B E E T C M W T F T P A G Q R O A I
E V C K T M D O C E R I B A G I F P J B
H W H N T S L K V X K L A H C E N I L I
C X E P H Y B E K Q U M R O F I N U Y U
N M F G L F U T H K Q T T I M R V Y A Q
```

BAG	CHEST PROTECTION	LINE CHALK
BALL	CLEATS	MITT
BASEBALL CAP	FIRST BASE	PANTS
BAT	HELMET	SCOREBOARD
BATTERS BOX	HOME PLATE	SECOND BASE
BATTING GLOVES	JERSEY	THIRD BASE
CATCHERS HELMET	KNEE SAVERS	UMPIRE
CATHERS MITT	LEG GUARDS	UNIFORM

DEFENSE

```
O A L L A B D E S S A P L I E W D E D A
V B F U C X C T O T A L C H A N C E S O
K T S I S S A D L E I F T U O L I X H E
V W O L X B U V W F X G S S H I F T N G
E J P E W I G V G S H I H X P C W D E A
A G L N R A H E M L B A S S I S T E S T
H J E H N Y T V R T P Q R J N J N Y S N
B P F I L U S X T U Y V L T R P J A C E
Y U T K Y C T C U O K S E E I Y A L Q C
V T F C Y K E E O X O I K T Y O O P T R
D O I V A K A N E W B G C G N X X S K E
G U E M L H L T K P N H Q I L P C G R P
D T L Y P Q I E I N E I K O D G E N E G
L J D B E J N R R I S L E O P S I H N
E H C F L K G F T D T E P S U D E N C I
I S R N P V C I S W X C K A B L V N T D
F C H O I G V E J S L O O B L X O I A L
T T R P R U C L O Y G N L D E E L J C E
H T W J T R D D I V V D M R P M G E K I
G O S H F G E H G K Y B W I L A D Q F F
I B K L H G T C Y T T A O H A R L O M U
R S L O J C X E G V F S O T Y K O O T P
V P A F I R S T B A S E X E Y F G B A J
M S X H O U R I M W A P O T S T R O H S
```

ASSIST · CATCHER · CAUGHT STEALING · CENTER FIELD · DOUBLE PLAY · ERROR · FIELDING PERCENTAGE · FIRST BASE · GOLD GLOVE · INNINGS PLAYED · LEFT FIELD · OUT · OUTFIELD ASSIST · PASSED BALL · PITCHER · PUTOUT · RIGHT FIELD · SECOND BASE · SHIFT · SHORTSTOP · STRIKE OUT · THIRD BASE · TOTAL CHANCES · TRIPLE PLAY

OFFENSE

```
H I T B Y P I T C H P A V D S L B S F G
D H O T V R E D N U O R G U X K I A E R
Q F G R U N S B A T T E D I N L O C Q K
C X T U S Q R I K M T F D J D A C R W H
U A I I H O M E R U N F U N R W E I V H
B G U J H A X P O A D H T E C J L F S T
B F X G U E P X P Y G P A S N J B I T O
U T D C H F S G V A I C E O D X U C O G
R U N I C T P A M G H F M L E D O E L W
U P L T I H S E B E Y A K S P B D F E I
I I T E R S S T D A L F A V R I K L N S
M G L O X P I O E S R B Q C T W R Y B G
L Q Y G L W N N D A N T X J V S T T A V
S I M A W E X N G O L U X Y Y E N M S P
S O Y U R B A I T L I I Q E M F T W E V
M E N R E R Y F V J E N N M S S S F Q W
D I O Y G W E N F R S X B G K G H Y K A
L R R V L L R J J O A E Y G D N W H C T
X C J O X K S D T H G U D E H A O K J B
H P L A T E A P P E A R A N C E Y C E A
G T Y W E G A R E V A G N I T T A B Q T
C V T N U B E C I F I R C A S B L K F V
Y Y K L A W L A N O I T N E T N I Y L L
A W D I T R E N S S E S A B L A T O T V
```

AT BAT	HIT	RUNS BATTED IN
BATTING AVERAGE	HIT BY PITCH	SACRIFICE BUNT
CAUGHT STEALING	HOME RUN	SACRIFICE FLY
DOUBLE	INTENTIONAL WALK	SINGLE
EXTRA-BASE HIT	LEFT ON BASE	STOLEN BASE
GAMES PLAYED	PLATE APPEARANCE	TOTAL BASES
GRAND SLAM	REACHED ON ERROR	TRIPLE
GROUNDER	RUN	WALK

SOLUTIONS

Name: _____

Baseball Teams Crossword Puzzle

Across
2. ST LOUIS
4. ARIZONA
6. CLEVELAND
8. LOS ANGELES
14. MINNESOTA
16. KANSAS CITY
19. PITTSBURGH
20. BOSTON
21. SAN DIEGO
22. HOUSTON
23. TAMPA BAY
24. BALTIMORE
25. TORONTO
26. MILWAUKEE
28. CHICAGO
29. SAN FRANCISCO
30. NEW YORK

Down
1. NEW YORK
3. CINCINNATI
5. TEXAS
7. DETROIT
9. PHILADELPHIA
10. SEATTLE
11. WASHINGTON
12. CHICAGO
13. OAKLAND
15. LOS ANGELES
17. ATLANTA
18. MIAMI
27. COLORADO

Name: _____

Baseball Word Search Puzzle 2

S T I R U P S R W P H C C C V H K
O U L J B L T S Q U E E Z E A C B
F Y F P C K R B X V Q L U N A U L
F W S Q A R A E O D N P Z P A O Q
I X P F I O N W T E Q U D Q M W K
H U I L Q D D I L E O I H W B G I
W B T S P I K E S K H A Z F T O V
H I B E Y P F W L E S D W B E U Y
J I A P S H D L Z D E V N X Q Y X
J A L C V E T E R A N A F M M O B
D I U N W H H T L F Q N N E F B E
R U B B E R C Q H T A C N A C V A
U K A R X H W T O A I E W T F C N
R E K C A B E M O C R B O B W G B
M A V O I Y E Z S P I X R A H S A
Q Y P U O S K C E D N O D L W V L
A C E F B I C O C M D R R U H A U

Ace
Advance
Beanball
Comebacker
Deeked
Meatball
Ondeck
Rubber
Spikes
Spitball
Squeeze
Stirups
Strand
Veteran
Whiff

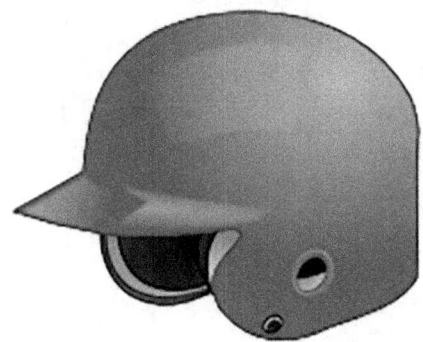

Name: _____

Baseball Word Search Puzzle 3

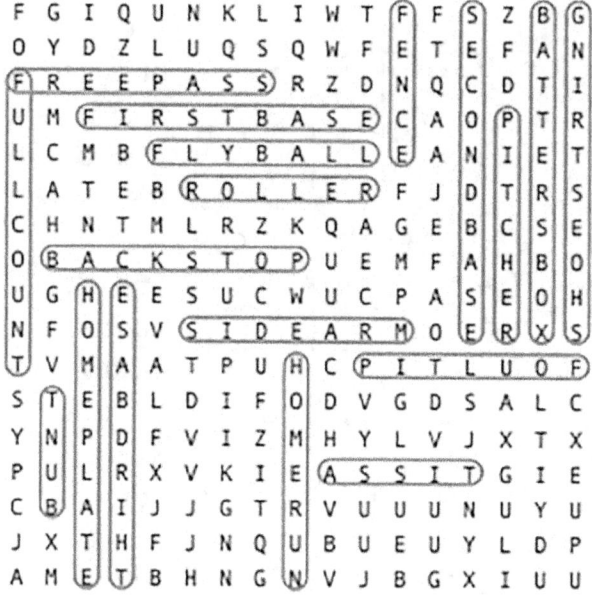

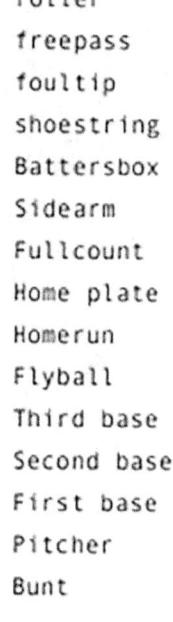

backstop
Fence
Assit
roller
freepass
foultip
shoestring
Battersbox
Sidearm
Fullcount
Home plate
Homerun
Flyball
Third base
Second base
First base
Pitcher
Bunt

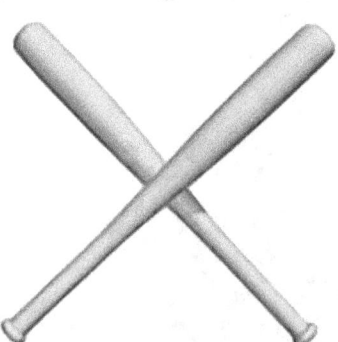

SPRING TRAINING PARKS (Solution)

```
J X R O G E R D E A N L X N T G X A T G
F N R E N N E R B N I E T S J S V Q T F
F D R S T J E V X L P Y Y G B U V T I V
S M O C E L Y O V V E L V A E N F T E U
U D N O M M A H M C O X S K X T T S D Y
R T A Q N Y N T F S R X U E N E E A B R
P G C Q S R M D A K I D H J A U V H S A
R K W F W M O R O X A T N M C H U Q D I
I J V S X W W D I P O K U X I L B U P E
S A L T R I V E R F I E L D S S Y W G E
E P L H C N A R K C A B L E M A C K Q K
E D E L E C T R I C P A R K T K Q Q W Y
I S J J K H T I M S D E X K U G P M Y O
E U L B T E J P E J D K T U M F H H A M
K K G A M E R I C A N F A M I L Y J D A
K D S C O T T S D A L E N N Y R D V O K
O L B A I D E P M E T I B T P N F S T O
L K Y B V S J J S L O A N P A R K T L H
I M A U H W G E R A C Y A B Q O Q N O O
K R A P R E V O L C H D O D M S O T O H
G K R A P L L A B D T K Y A C X F H C M
Y G M R P J D H H N D J N A Q N W U A A
J X X M C H A R L O T T E O I W O O V X
S D W T L G O O D Y E A R T A R F R K Q
```

MLB TEAM NAMES (Solution)

```
P T M M T M S T N A I G Y T W P K Q W Q
I H F A B V D T L D J X A A U L I X M O
C U I H T X E A S C D E N R N S F T R N
T D T L Y H R P U L W P A M E K S I U P
I W Q Q L X L B B S C T M V H E E G S H
K G A H O I S E N M D S A W T C I E H B
O S T S P E E A T S A R W A V H T R S Q
W R D R O L I S T I B I R S E H S S G L
B E I K B D L N N Y C I L N P O E E C M
R G R O N G A B J L P S H F V R X H T U
T D E I L I P T B G S Y A J E U L B V H
O O H U G E F K S S F B Y J G C P U R C
W D W A C S S Q S T L U R S J U F A O P
D T S J V N F S K J D A L T P E N D Y W
M W M N Q I G K C S A A N I R G S H A H
M I G G T L X J A C N K H O E H G D L I
V N D P D R S E B I K B B L I U G Y S T
U S T R F A B A D K T L S O M T M W F E
I T H W T M L R N C T M Y S Y B A Q C S
R Y T N S E A O O G N W E X M R E N L O
Y D N H J C G C M L I U I T U C X K I X
H G S E X M O Y A Q P H R T S M I Y D N
U C M H T G L V I T V T Y U J R H K Y I
N Y A B P Y L E D M A A N H F D Q B W D
```

SCORING TERMS (Solution)

```
D S E L G N I S D L E I F N I Y K F H I
H F A X D G U S D Y V S A Q G L A B P P D
F C J A S C B U P K F Q P X R F G R C R
P A T E A T R D V J V Y W P O E W A C O
O N M I A L C E V W I H D O U C N I N P
Y P X A P B T R I I V W U H N I F C F P
F U U O H Y U R V U S L C N D F G V E E
F Y F E D K B C U F B S V U R I G M L D
I C H T L C F T P B U N T R U R A A P B
E G R C C U B L I U X R E E L C P W I A
L F O A T V R C E H Q H F M E A J U R L
D L R T T I C Y W M G I E O D S Q D T L
E K R Q R I P J L R O N V H O X X N E A
R J E W J J H D A F I H D O U B L E L C
S P Y K A J H N L L D A L W B U R N U T
C Y Y X J L D B E I W L O A L X I F R W
H W E E I S K H E C W I E F E E N I D E
O E E L L G T U G L P V X I Y T E M N A
I R A A P N I G X K G D B O F U S C U X
C K M L W I P V J R L N R S O N Y O O H
E S B O A D R U H D Q A I L G Y I X R B
H V D S I F P T X B P V B S P Y L O G I
L I N S I D E T H E P A R K F R N U N W
W A L K O F F V R B Y H O M B D W J R L
```

RECENT AMERICAN LEAGUE ALL-STARS (Solution)

```
T W E N D L E Y N O G G A I C R A G R K
A V D A J M W W X U Y Y E G G J M I O U
C K S O N A G A O R C O R R E A J G H X
S U I G E F A L L B O G A E R T S L L Y
J P J A I I L I Q S D E D G O T M W I S
Q D D L M B L S T J H K O A E Y R H E G
P L B U E R O R U O V B K C Y P E J F R
K E Y H S A I E O W L O M D E E T O P L
A I Y D B N B U R N A E D R X H T W W F
L F K L Q T N D T C N L E X S X E K S A
T I K R D L O L G O E Z N W B C H Y D D
U R I K D E G Q M Y R G H P L E C S H G
V R E Z E Y G U E R R E R O O Q I S Y E
E E C I U B U O Y F N S Q G R A B T N H
L M B Y Q N I U W U O H P E H O S S L I
W E B L U X I Y V S S L A Y B A R D N U
I O D F G I B N E I R F S D B E C L G I
P B R Y R R L G O P E D Q O V A V P X K
E J N V T M D E J S D W D E N Z K R J D
N G W R Y U V Y I S N N D K U H H M P O
R U J W J D K M T I A C P R S K I J S N
P W Z E D N A N R E H B C S Y Y Y M X D
X H W P Z E R I M A R X L S N I L L U M
F K N P U M E M A R T I N E Z J S J V L
```

RECENT NATIONAL LEAGUE ALL-STARS (Solution)

```
V V R E B R A W H C S G B V J O G F F X
S W C A S T E L L A N O S D O Q H I I K
W Q R E I Z A R F V S U A D K C S H Q H
M F R E E M A N C C T T A Y D A D V V S
M V F I D S W W D F W N T D S Y L X O F
U N I K W E H F V W E A Q S G E O C T C
N U N B M L G P F R W Y L F E A N Q U O
C S Q V Y W J K A X C J N Y V K Y R M B
Y K T X S H L S R M E M I P L H E N L M
U V W A M B P B W H F S Y J O E R G A F
K B B T N H A L E I X F C V K S W X E T
R A E K G P N N Y T N D W O C X E C R A
I L J W A B I I F X T K R O B D D Y A Y
D B M P C K L A E E D S E O F A E B E L
M I Y Y U G O B C E Q F T R F L R C D O
R E N I N D M J V G F F X S W W C Q A R
E S O B A H H T R O W E N O R C A J V P
N O R R B R D U A N A R V A E Z C R H F
R N U Y F O T O S Y K V L H H E I K C U
U P L A J C O D A H C A M T D V R U K Q
T P W N Y A U H V R Q H B K G B O M D J
D V P T T S H W G F H M N L P R P H R W
G S I T A T X D S S D W I M J F Y V Y B
L Y O S S R B M P S H U M U V W S F S O
```

MOST VALUABLE TRADING CARDS (Solution)

```
P N L R S L M Q V R L Q H W V F R R W N
S M A I L L I W J A O O S R D G K E J R
Y C C N Y W R S J I L B U X S I F L F L
G Y C F T H Y O H I J F I Y Y U N T E E
B C X E J H I G A A M X K N R O E N P Y
R F K N D E U M E Q M S Q D S L Y A D K
M U S I A L H A Q L S A J S C O G M H E
B I A J I E O W J Q F A T H D P N W S Q
H E T N E M E L C I S N P H A V H Y X Y
R L W C Q G V O Q K E C K F E A O M E P
B S K I O D H D U U Y D N R O W R D L B
K N W X Y O S G L R O U A T P M S O B O
N U W E E X T F U Y T P L O L J F O N W
K M S X H I P V L O V O P J T O S N N O
W M E L N T G E T T G S V F D H U F R K
T R G E M T A A E E J N U R M N N K T F
W H I C R O O M M U E O E R V S R X W A
E M A N J C J M L C D G H B J O Q U T P
S L P L Y D I M A G G I O Y H N S D J E
N C C O E Q K P F U S E D H T K Y I U V
J N U B U Y L I G E H R I G U D A E N W
G N K E B T X F E G X B F A R G M G N P
G Q S L S O P H E X P K M R E N G A W L
X O U H H U C F L J A C K S O N S P X Q
```

TAKE ME OUT TO THE BALL GAME (Solution)

```
C D F S Q O U V U E P A G T K A Y I U U
B Q G L W U A D B N E V J T B M X C W F
U Y E N R S P T A G B R B K C A B E N J
W U V K M T P I W S R P H P H I K R V T
A B T T N Y L S P F X G S T M R P F V U
C R O W D M Y B G S B H R A E W T O V M
V M P R N R Y X A Y C M B O O N E N C D
F H A O K J A B R M O C N E L E K E X J
V D T P E I K E S T U N A E P C Q V S A
P N Y Q C M L J P E L D D O A H W E S A
W G J T U R A V O U D C F J J E K K Q Y
H P K W L O S H M K T E U P R I F D B H
I I I C E G M T S G U Q G Y R H T U S T
W F M M K C N Y R I O G S T B I Y A L N
P T O A P W T W F E Q E S A E L Q S L E
O H Y U E H A C O W T X T M B E C S T V
E G H O T T R A G Q Q C Q E O T O J A E
I H O Q V W C R A Y H E H G M Q O D P S
B E W I N V K E M N U V G R N V K O L R
B K T B E G U T E A G E F H G I J T R O
L I V U J L A M O I P R L J H B N S T O
L V H Y B K N M A L X L J R K S M N Y E
A I Q O E H F R N R E F T Y E H T E I E
B I B X M T Q B Q N P L P P O X P M V E
```

NATIONAL LEAGUE CITIES (Solution)

```
S P X A T D Y N O T G N I H S A W D P U
A B M O Q W S S J H G R U B S T T I P H
N M N G G B E E L X F C R K S M R G L S
D I P F D S R L U T F D M Y O A C G C T
I L N R T Q D E H C K H Q H T K L A I L
E W M E T S A G B A D N D E P V R K M O
G A M T W L P N A C B Y S F V D M Q S U
O U G R J P P A K E O H P G I C I U E I
W K Q V A P N S G W J S W N D R A Y J S
Q E U U K G N O K U E O A P M Q M Q V F
N E E H K G T L A H P L F T T B I E D A
E B R M O C H F L L S L S E I L L I H P
W G Q W R H C H I C A G O W W F R S X B
Y K A I H P L E D A L I H P V O G R B Y
O S R E W E R B L B H Y Y B R A V E S N
R K V A V D A J A S E X U E K S D E R A
K Q A R U F B O T N S J R L O O D F E T
C D M S O V E O L M N S S S M X D X O I
E D M Y B A F B A R I V H G R U Y L T O
H R Y K V U A V N D L S R E G D O D A N
J A E F B F C M T S R U T W H D P U J A
K S V O D Y X U A V A M V X W P H T S L
E Y Q J W B Q I R L M F K N D C T R E S
G L X G Y J Q V I T A N N I C N I C N K
```

108

AMERICAN LEAGUE CITIES (Solution)

```
F H T I G E R S A O X T R Q S U M E G I
Q U Y F A F T F K K O O X O E E A M Y A
S F V M Q C M R E H S R L S G T R E L R
E D H D P A O K F D D O J K H G I M S A
A Y C S T Y O N H J E N Q T M B N W V N
T U L M W V H T A Y R T K D K E E U H C
T E O E M U A J I I M O R C F R R Q C S
L F N D P M X L Q X C U H O R G S N K N
E U K J P K H L L J S R O P I A O C B A
W R A A J U J F Y C D O U J L T Y K U I
B K B B B Q B N C R H O S A I C V V S D
A A P S L A Y O R N A F T W C L Q V Y R
Y N B O S T O N L K R S O R T S A O A U
J S J U I F B I L Y F O N X C D A R J U
E A O E J S M A P S A O C B I Q Y I E G
U S N G C S N F D B C N D S V S G O U L
J C J J A D C J D N T N K J A P O L L W
D I D J M C V I A R A Y S E S F Q E B A
X T D S A Q I R T L D J S I E P M S W Y
J Y E A E L M H E E U N Q B V S C C Q Y
A C Q E M L I V C E L O Q R F L J P P I
D N T O F O E O W J K H P M U A R Q V F
D V X L V L D O A W H I T E S O X E Y H
R B R U C W E R O M I T L A B S W E D F
```

MLB GOLD GLOVE AWARD WINNERS (Solution)

```
H Q G V O R L X D H W K U N P O O N K Y
P O W E R L U S S I A O G A L X U Q R O
S C A M P A N E L L A C R S D N O B N K
H H I R J M P G I R T S B E M B Y T I F
E U V H C E L N O P I O O I C H E N I T
R H B K P Q E D V T M A Z E R O S K I S
D M B S F R R T R E N O F G M X T U P I
X A P Y B I L B T W B B I O W U R X R R
O Y K X G Q L N D O E Q F T P O Z G O B
H S K U M O V B I S N Y Y T N R E X B O
M D E S L T G C M H C W M R X P M B I Z
E Z I P X L V D H I H T E X S U S L N U
E I E A X E F H C G C M I T V P K E S F
N J C Q H G W W S O L N M Y N W I X O R
H E R N A N D E Z Q E P C K I E Q J N R
G R A F B R P C A P A R I C I O M G R B
L E E H R G X F O Z E H C N A S H E Y T
B G X T B R U R N L R Q A Y C H V I L U
P N W I F H A J F E S B V S H F M Y C C
I A N M N I S F O E E B Y O I B H D S R
Q L I S M D I G V D N G O R D O N T U M
X E V X X U F O Y A O D B B X U D D A M
N B W W H I T E V Y J C G R E I N K E Q
K Q Y M P K E R U T R R J E G M Y P V W
```

GREATEST HITTERS (Solution)

```
S E I E Q N W M G L G V U B A E W S X T
L G A I J M F T O V U H S O X N F C P N
G M G L A I S U M L E A U X E Y T D N M
O V W U M C A C G N I E J K M L E R Y I
L S Y K H X O F D O X T P J G S H X V C
M A Y S D B X E W U F I O T O H B P K N
P I P M B F R D W I R K G R H S K Q R E
X R W D Q S J R K E N H T T X G Y K E I
P R I P O C F M W R Y A A R O N V O N O
G C K N C T E M L T M C B I A J D I G Y
J S S G F O Q R T L R H V K E C D G A M
H E M K W I I I I E O W B N V F C G W P
X L E A F B R K C B D M A T D B N I V R
C O Z C O T G D R A R Q N N Y W G B U B
D N R R O K A E Y E I G S F D A V T D J
K S T V E L Q D R O Q G O E F Q H F G J
O M S K L K L M F Y U K N K F O Y B E Y
H N A G N S A I R S E X L D I M R T K P
F G Y X G R D E N J Z N B J G O E K T X
R J G N N O W I P S L P L R C R R B C D
A T B Y W N B O S S U P D K D B B V V I
T U O Y P U J O L S N I Q D W C Y J O S
R X T X P A L M E I R O K N C F M S E C
W Y P R I M T V H T G U T S U Z U K I I
```

GREATEST PITCHERS (Solution)

```
E E B L W S A B A T H I A I U A E C U F
A L E U Z N E L A V F Q Y A D A L L A H
R Q C T I N K A X C G C R Q J J M Y W S
J P K M I W Y N G N I L L I H C S C J G
X Q F V R Y A N P Q M G L J J P J X C C
Q G A Q J M Y S S N P X A F U O K T Y J
V L B F D P E L D D O O A W S H E S W C
G M H K O V U D Z Q M S X R S A S C A B
E A C O W S M E K D E U N O Q F M G H U
F D J K J G N E R O D U P H E G U U S M
D J E J G I R Y V D G R P L O C F J R G
V R Y G T Q S O A S R W L D H J U X E A
G Q E R B D X M V E T E Q N P O Q K K R
G Q A D A M U T Z E R B X F B O V M L N
C M X L N O J R L S Y P N O T L R A C E
Q D E D S A E W J R I X Q T N H M P F R
E V T G I H L N F N B L S X P N I P S M
D Y J Q C T D R J I R X A B L A G T T I
J R T S M G C B E Y A W R R T H T K R Q
Z T L O M S W W Q V C O E J A V H Q E K
E J M C S E A V E R A N V F J O L M B B
B N H S F C X F H R V G I H J G N U O Y
N N S W B E H D Q W E M R B W Q E M R L
I E O J G M R K S N E M E L C J K E R K
```

ABC'S (Solution)

```
Q J F M G A X A S F K P T F L O P A O U
Y Q H C S W T X B A S E S L O A D E D M
W U V P R E V Y I Q I L O I Y M O K E P
J N D Y M L D L L A B N A E B E R K A X
X M V Y T V V R P A K D H B B W V V X G
F F L C E N T E R F I E L D E R P H X O
C U R V E B A L L C G G P Y O B T A B O
D S L M L I V R P N G A M A J D G V I R
B S R E A K G V I V C T O N C P D I J P
E I E L W A H N T T L B U N Y K R I F M
S I T P U V N C N G Q A H H R H Y C G E
A Y T J I U I A C Y Q T C E B O R U A C
B C A E R A C R Y F M T H E U Q H D T R
V S B E Y X K D J F A C L X L F C L H R
S E S S A D P E W C T L T E L V H B L N
S A P A S S I S T A A P O T P X A X E T
B D X D P B P R C B C F J A E M M C T N
S Q E E H T R N E F F H I B N L P U E U
H R E T T I H H C T U L C P L F I Q K B
B K D L E I F R E T N E C H N M O E X S
M B F F O X H A W E X X K U R Q N C O O
R J P S T L L A B E S A B L E A Y D C Q
L D G K J W N K B U L C F G A I U M P G
L Y I K G B I Q N G R L Q L B B J H A U
```

STADIUM FOODS (Solution)

```
X K D R V Q G I H Y S H U T H D G N P B
J P S A I G X I T F R X R A S O M M P R
U W P V G O D T O H L A M U C S C W A H
K V N H I C R Q L D I B N A R T O K D T
O Q R S C A A P S L U F I E U W T N O R
N A R G E N R A M R L V G W D C T I S U
A H V Q C D X I G O C N D L R P O P F G
C L O V R Y X E W J I J A A E E N U H O
H N S P E I R E I F Q L C X L A C P W Y
O O C X A P R N N P N K K U R N A F G N
D U L J M S T E A A E V X T J U N Q X E
O I T N E R K H G R D P E D U T D O J Z
X K J E K C S C J R M Y I B C S Y W Q O
M J D J I O A A A E U U U C F A K X E R
E S B H K M C C A E D B Q A K Y T S W F
D Y C W N K O H J M G W E K M L I B N U
C N C F S B R X Q J D W K S Y X E W R F
O Q Y M P Q K D U D V C O T E E K S O J
R J M U G E L B B U B K T R R E S X C X
N U E G P T X U H C I W D N A S H Q P B
D X A S O I Y C M T M O E H C J S C O C
O T M G K W A T E R H C W D O O D Q P E
G P R E T Z E L S J K B A R B E C U E Q
J M X U S K C I T S A L L E R A Z Z O M
```

111

TEAM NICKNAMES (Solution)

```
B I J N S B X G W S E R D A P V S D L F
R E C N Y O A T S D E R M J W U C S L L
S U J S C F P Y X S V R E K U R N E M S
Y U B Y X N X R M X G J E A M G H I E H
A Q O P A H X G G V S D E X S R S K M C
R A S C A R D I N A L S J E R Y T C Y D
N W F W C Y O C G T S A V R A O R O D Q
A C R E N G X I E I U A K J M R Y R M V
T B M S E T A R I P R K E Q P I H X R S
I P I I M W T D U B L U O I N O E H A R
O H S E J W R I G O L D D G F L M N F E
N T T I Q K V A G B L A B E O E D Y R G
A S C Q V L M M J L F T R N S S Q P Q I
L L C U B S L O T Y E H I V N F V P N T
S A N G A L S N S C G L A E D F R F Q C
U Y D X M W R D R S W E P S R E G D O D
L O H U S A A B E I E T M T W I N S S D
K R Q X N S I A N S I I B H S J U V V V
R T W G F L T C I N C C I U N I V A Y A
O J E B F E T K R I P S G D D P P M V M
L R I R A G L S A L B M S R E W E R B K
S Q G Y A N C P M R J A U W F Y R W G W
S D M L Y A J W M A R S N A I D N I S S
L U Q N C W R F Q M K F S W V W S Y S T
```

4 LETTER BASEBALL WORDS (Solution)

```
L N P U G E D T K W Y M J X V N F G B E
B P P N H O L N M L P I P B R N G W I B
S A D O S G D S T T U F Q D D R A C Q W
K C U N B E T C O X U O Q Q D F M H I R
I C E R S V C R I A F B F S J D A B B T
N S X A F D L L N G O W Q K X T I Q Q R
T M B Q Y S K L P E X L V P B F I R G J
C F B N D J C C F H N S X U L R N W C W
M R C D G L I E X P L I L I A A L B Y H
Q T K N P L A V U R A C N E L B Y C R J
I M L F U A F F B P J H G O X A E Q J T
H T A A C H R Q T K X J Y L M L M M F O
R P W B Y X O K F Y O F N Q L L A H T S
W E L O F C D M W Q D Y X P V O G I C Y
U M G E J C X J D O E S N E U S U U A N
X O K C E D C S O V G N Q T H T U N L U
J H Q Q I L O S A F D W S J T E G L L L
U I G Y I K F S I F S T R I L E H L I F
B H W N S P J C W G R K M G O L I K Y A
I G U L V W H N W N Q B O L S J T N J P
X E A E X X K M N I E Q W R E C S E R P
D M B T F D B B B N H N M Y B U H W C S
J R D Y K B U N T I N F I C X A S W D B
K P T B P S I L V K E G J L F K A G G A
```

FUNNY NICKNAMES (Solution)

```
L V O L W V K S K C U D R E B B U R S L
S E I N O P E L B M U R C V O X T D Y W
F T D T W N C X V L J C R W O G A D O M
M Y B J E M S N D I U S A S K E M B B U
T R H I L L C A T S R E A R H K F J W V
D E G R U S D N I W A U W R J I L E O K
W N J H O O K S U S Q E E A W T X W C S
T K E V B F N B L A B M E O H D G E E K
T I N C A P S D S F M O L N N O T C C K
F S G I P N O R I A N T O G E J O T A B
S R A Y X O S J H K H K A R X G P S P A
T A T R G C D O B X O W Q A D X S H S M
I I S A W P A X U A S J D S B I Q R J U
U L E W U H D U B N I A R S Y T E A M D
C R L H B H W I A C D E H H J X S U I C
S A D I D S A Q H P L S S O U P D U A A
I I O D S A R M M L K E G P A M I H E T
B D O E H P C J I C X S A P L O O N S S
K E P H R Q G R G E R J I E L B O Y O L
C R D Q T K D X Q G S T T R L B Y D P N
M S O C P B D X U J A S J S L F J F C A
B Q S S P S R E K C E P D O O W S R T N
B M D P M I R H S O B M U J S K C N F C
T R A S H P A N D A S E H S W K I W F F
```

STADIUM SPONSORS (Solution)

```
C H A S E U R B E V A U S H P P G U E U
E O O C T E P S E L O I R O D G E K L X
N T T D I A M E T U N I M A D G R V A I
O J Y E O V A I E X P A V A C P M U E O
P C X W C K B R H G E P I X J I Q J G A
B N A C I R E M A T A E R G X G T V V C
O Y M Y A T A N D T T A R G E T F I M I
J M R A L U L L E C S U D Q F J Y K B R
Y T N A M F F U A K V F C E I X V U L E
C V X R V D B A S R E H V P L V I R Q M
N S H O L U T P P N C F N H E A V E Q O
T L F U T C E Q W S T W K C B I L N B C
R A O F V E R A U J W A R K O W R R H N
O N O S G V Y B Q A E Q O N L D U U M R
P O I N J I T U K L J H H H G W B T S C
I I Y E S S A W Y Y B T Q Y S R L H R U
C T J Z Y S F N P B F T Q F N I W F E S
A A D I S E V N B E C P O I R G D M G K
N N M T M R E J N L R B C S L L N B O M
A A Y I Q G H J E S H E E B A E E Q R X
V E E C G O Y M F R O S F D C Y N F C G
F S N I L R A M B O C S A N F S T F P C
P V D U T P V F B O N D S J J I L O A F
I R W R I N X F I C K M G X D V D P Q U
```

113

"S" WORDS (Solution)

```
N O M A A I S U J J P S C M U W F L L E
L A E T S G H B F X A O S P O L U Q U L
S L S W G F O P G W M C G R E G G U L S
Y S Q C C X R C K D O N E B Z Y V S B F
E K I R T S T T I R R N C T E B Y A Y F
M E B N W C S B E L N A I E E I Q V T E
Y O Y M Q E T B C C B S F W U X E E U Q
W F N S F Y O Q Q L S M I G Q R Q S O D
S X G T T A P P E C N U R M S I J D T H
T J R N R O A A A K X I C S V G N U U X
R V J D I C L R D S S D A S R O C E H J
E D X A T N O E E I L A S D C H U S S R
T C J N G U I H N H I T F E E O I C X W
C S H I F T T A I U D S S K O G E R L H
H G O X J S N Q R E E S O F T B A L L V
B L B S E I R E S T O Y U T H I G G A A
K L B A S N E B V D G O S C F J I Y B Q
H M M C E L V X M L N N T I L O L J T P
J Q O N V V X W N V P A I P K Y N L I H
S R Y N T O G I W F R M X R J V R U P M
E A V B R O H U K C Q Q W A P J T C S W
F S N D O I S A S S R J A J D S H M F Y
E Q X C P S W I T C H H I T T E R L K M
G T K E S W L N C R Q R A V W U O G L U
```

MASCOTS (Solution)

```
N I C U R I K J H K E V B K N J U M D N
W T T M R M E T U F G V O A E E D N X A
S L U G G E R R R V Q X M N M F J A O S
Y X H C E E R C S O Q L B S T H T A L C
B X J L U A V V L D E T U E R N N M A I
X Q U D M G H F Y R W F M G E F P R E T
D N O M Y A R I R I X B S A W P V O S A
P A B Q K T Y A R B I L U S E K R S U N
L N J B T V B R V D V N O U R M E I O A
D Y L G O O E P Q E W N E A B X P E L H
J T I R K G H P P R J E B S E M P R L P
I T Y B N T X T O F N S B E I M A E E E
R I N I P O C Y F P R G R H N C G D F I
H K D Q A L Q T I B R O T T R C A I K L
A J K X J W E S T R U Y U Y E P C C P L
D D A R O B Q M Y V R D H C B R E W B I
A T A C B O B E H T R E T X A B V D U H
W L B C R O D A H C U L S K C A B D N P
X P Q B I L L Y T H E M A R L I N G J T
O A R P C E S O O M R E N I R A M X K G
M W R U B H P D B N W W M R J Q D B H X
S S C V J V T O R R A P E T A R I P W J
S K R E D I L S E Q U Q Q L W V I K F T
R A I R F G N I G N I W S J H S Y U W R
```

POSITIONS (Solution)

```
U B H C A O C E S A B T S R I F N P J O
V J K C K F D L E I F T H G I R L V E B
D Y B E L L L H C A O C G N I H C T I P
E N R S R E F D R I H T C N Q V U O G A
S A U R J F P I T C H E R C H V E S T R
I T I X B T S H I T T I N G C O A C H Y
G P M K E F T M D G O A S S E C O N D T
N E A A N I A A F O L U U H R D B B P C
A R N Q C E R G L D K D I A A F A D L G
T E A O H L T L C P C Q N F I S N M G E
E H G S C D I C R K F J U T E Y A J C N
D C E L O J N D E U R J J R C U F C N E
H T R U A S G S Y N M E U F A V D I R R
I I R R C D P O A D T N H M S T S T O A
T P S E H T I F N J N E I C K L N U N L
T F T T C S T C R E D F R U T T X H U M
E E S T K R C L R A W O S F N A D C B A
R I M A S I H O O Q S P G S I V C A T N
E L Y B L F E S W O C K F V W E N O G A
U E U T E P R E X M Q O M M C H L C X G
L R Y W B O T R Y A K B H E F U O D H E
M H C A O C E S A B D R I H T H H U H R
G G B F J J F V S H O R T S T O P X Q A
X R H C A O C N E P L L U B K P X X I B
```

PITCHERS (Solution)

```
S D S R E T T I L P S R U U W K J G W G
A H K I F R U S K D A F S Q Y W P S N A
P V U K W H A X F C E E P H U S Y Y R C
L L A B W E R C S U T B T Y W X F Y J L
T U O D N U O R G R O P P V S B J N O X
B L L Y Q Q S R J V D Y E V A E V S A W
X U K R E D I L S E T W R L K E S P N C
L L A B K R O F D B L E L W M H U A J R
I M A C Q G G V I A B M F H R C C K N H
N U W T C T I K E L I R K E H V U Y J I
S N E I G J O V U L E C K K W T J R A T
H U V S T R I K E N H N S L D Y H O B B
U K R T P K X D P F I M X A Q U X O D Y
T N U B Y E V I U S W U Y B A A I F Q P
O U C F O U R S E A M F A S T B A L L I
U C E D L X O E G C C R V C H U N M X T
T K L A S V P O N N U C E F G J H V J C
T L K J A C V R A K T U M I I J C C W H
M E C Y V F A O H L T Y L F A J E V V W
Y B U X E K R V C A E A N S D G S F M I
S A N J B D S X W W R A P B X A C G K N
J L K O W G A I L C W L V K E X T P N K
Q L L E L L A B T S A F M A E S O W T W
S W I L D P I T C H N T B C J V G Y C E
```

EQUIPMENT (Solution)

```
F Q S D X G T J K N E E S A V E R S Y V
T H I R D B A S E M Q S W C V U S P H E
S M L J X A G I L M P H A U C A U N H S
S K H N N S H D I C V M S B R H T E W A
A I E C B E G G R B Q D L P T G N C Y B
B L G T B B A H L A D G J V M S L E B D
D F T A N A T M Y L O O U P A E R D X N
P K T S P L E P D L V B P T A S O I V O
N U I P Q L M S A K E U E T B A O C F C
O L M E Y C L I E N L Q S R M K C O N E
I R S L E A E T Q V T E O V O A J M O S
T W R H S P H D B S O S G V E C J V T O
C F E O R G S H G D Y L W G A Q S A T C
E X H M E C R Y L U M G G W U S G C Q T
T A T E J Q E R H C P U E G T A M D N C
O F A P S H H I G P I W P O N A R N M R
R U C L F K C K K Y Q F H A F I B D O M
P K S A B A T T E R S B O X R U T O S Q
T K K T O W A A A I E E R I P M U T I G
S R B E E T C M W T F T P A G Q R O A I
E V C K T M D O C E R I B A G I F P J B
H W H N T S L K V X K L A H C E N I L I
C X E P H Y B E K Q U M R O F I N U Y U
N M F G L F U T H K Q T T I M R V Y A Q
```

DEFENSE (Solution)

```
O A L L A B D E S S A P L I E W D E D A
V B F U C X C T O T A L C H A N C E S O
K T S I S S A D L E I F T U O L I X H E
V W O L X B U V W F X G S S H I F T N G
E J P E W I G V G S H I H X P C W D E A
A G L N R A H E M L B A S S I S T E S T
H J E H N Y T V R T P J R J N J N Y S N
B P F I L U S X T U Y V L T R P J A C E
Y U T K Y C T C U O K S E E I Y A L Q C
V T F C Y K E E O X O I K T Y O O P T R
D O I V A K A N E W B G C G N X X S K E
G U E M L H L T K P N H Q I L P C G R P
D T L Y P Q I E I N E I K O D G E N E G
L J D B E J N R R I S L E O P S I H N
E H C F L K G F T D T E P S U D E N C I
I S R N P V C I S W X C K A B L V N T D
F C H O I G V E J S L O O B L X O I A L
T T R P R U C L O Y G N L D E E L J C E
H T W J T R D D I V V D M R P M G E K I
G O S H F G E H G K Y B W I L A D Q F F
I B K L H G T C Y T T A O H A R L O M U
R S L O J C X E G V F S O T Y K O O T P
V P A F I R S T B A S E X E Y F G B A J
M S X H O U R I M W A P O T S T R O H S
```

OFFENSE (Solution)

```
H I T B Y P I T C H P A V D S L B S F G
D H O T V R E D N U O R G U X K I A E R
Q F G R U N S B A T T E D I N L O C Q K
C X T U S Q R I K M T F D J D A C R W H
U A I I H O M E R U N F U N R W E I V H
B G U J H A X P O A D H T E C J L F S T
B F X G U E P X P Y G P A S N J B I T O
U T D C H F S G V A I C E O D X U C O G
R U N I C T P A M G H F M L E D O E L W
U P L T I H S E B E Y A K S P B D F E I
I I T E R S S T D A L F A V R I K L N S
M G L O X P I O E S R B Q C T W R Y B G
L Q Y G L W N N D A N T X J V S T T A V
S I M A W E X N G O L U X Y Y E N M S P
S O Y U R B A I T L I I Q E M F T W E V
M E N R E R Y F V J E N N M S S S F Q W
D I O Y G W E N F R S X B G K G H Y K A
L R R V L L R J J O A E Y G D N W H C T
X C J O X K S D T H G U D E H A O K J B
H P L A T E A P P E A R A N C E Y C E A
G T Y W E G A R E V A G N I T T A B Q T
C V T N U B E C I F I R C A S B L K F V
Y Y K L A W L A N O I T N E T N I Y L L
A W D I T R E N S S E S A B L A T O T V
```

117

www.ingramcontent.com/pod-product-compliance
Lightning Source LLC
Chambersburg PA
CBHW060325130626
46553CB00003B/926